D0971521

"The stories Thomas tells are inspiring, colorful, vast, and personal. He captures the fear of the early AIDS epidemic, the infighting among cancer groups lobbying for federal research dollars, and the joy of seeing your national service agenda embraced by the next president. Best of all, Thomas demonstrates why the fight is worth it. Thomas's career is more than a lesson: It's an inspiration."

—*Patti Solis Doyle, CNN contributor*
and presidential campaign manager

"*Helping the Good Do Better* chronicles the aspirational vision, authentic values, and tenacious strategies that led me to partner with Tom and the Sheridan Group as the main policy & advocacy consultancy for the ASBC. Our organization is committed to the 'Triple Bottom Line' of people, planet, and profit."

—*Hammad Atassi, CEO, American Sustainable Business Council*

"I read *Helping the Good Do Better* in one sitting. Packed with vivid stories and practical tips for both citizens who care and committed change agents, Sheridan makes a compelling argument for the essential role of advocacy in any effort to improve communities. The insightful commentary, hard-won lessons, and tools contained in *Helping the Good Do Better* are incredibly relevant for this generation of citizen entrepreneurs asking 'What can I do?'"

—*Cheryl Dorsey, CEO, Echoing Green*

"Sheridan makes a much-needed contribution with his new book. Most significantly for me, Tom offers those of us who straddle the applied and academe a better understanding of the theoretical foundations of advocacy so that it can be captured and communicated to students of government and political science everywhere."

—*Patrick Griffin, academic director, Public Affairs and*
Advocacy Institute, American University

"Sheridan opens an enjoyable and insightful window into his work on behalf of Americans who deserve better. Through engaging stories, he reminds us that our government has great power to do good. In our era of highly partisan politics, Sheridan boldly asserts that 'the non-profit sector needs to offer leadership that brings the American public together.'"—*John Staud, PhD, executive director, ACE Program, University of Notre Dame*

"At last, there is a true bible for how nonprofits can effect real transformative change. I was a witness to many of these stories—from the front lines of the AIDS epidemic in Atlanta to the White House. Tom's brand of pragmatism and political savvy might occasionally ruffle feathers, but he fights to win with the clear understanding that when you fight for those who can't fight for themselves the stakes are always higher. However, these pages bring those fights into perspective with his signature honest, humorous 'Irish storytelling.' Here is a book that tells you how a good guy finally won, and taught countless advocates how to win in the process." —*Sandy Thurman, White House AIDS Czar (Clinton Administration, 1997–2001)*

"For four score and two years, I've been a witness to a generation of social change and I know what it takes to take on the big issues and win. Tom is wise, disciplined, tough, strategic, and deeply committed to American Idealism and the promise it still holds for the great task of citizenship. This book passes the baton and inspires the reader to carry on."
—*former U.S. Senator Harris Wofford, author of* Of Kennedy and Kings

Helping the Good Do Better

HOW A WHITE HAT LOBBYIST
ADVOCATES FOR SOCIAL CHANGE

Thomas F. Sheridan

TWELVE

NEW YORK BOSTON

Twelve
Hachette Book Group
1290 Avenue of the Americas, New York, NY 10104
twelvebooks.com
twitter.com/twelvebooks

First Edition: June 2019

Twelve is an imprint of Grand Central Publishing. The Twelve name and logo are trademarks of Hachette Book Group, Inc.

The publisher is not responsible for websites (or their content) that are not owned by the publisher.

The Hachette Speakers Bureau provides a wide range of authors for speaking events. To find out more, go to www.hachettespeakersbureau.com or call (866) 376-6591.

Library of Congress Cataloging-in-Publication Data
Names: Sheridan, Thomas F., author.
Title: Helping the good do better : how a white hat lobbyist advocates for social change / by Thomas Sheridan.
Description: First edition. | New York : Twelve, 2019. | Includes index.
Identifiers: LCCN 2018052467| ISBN 9781538700167 (hardcover) | ISBN 9781549149511 (audio download) | ISBN 9781538700150 (ebook)
Subjects: LCSH: Social change--United States. | Social action--United States. | United States--Social policy. | Sheridan, Thomas F. | Lobbyists--United States--Biography.
Classification: LCC HN59.2 .S5 2019 | DDC 306.0973--dc23
LC record available at https://lccn.loc.gov/2018052467

ISBNs: 978-1-5387-0016-7 (hardcover), 978-1-5387-0015-0 (ebook)

Printed in the United States of America

LSC-C

10 9 8 7 6 5 4 3 2 1

To change makers: the individuals in the world who see problems and injustices and dedicate themselves to solving them. You know who you are, and I am one of you!

To my husband, Vince Walsh, and the Sheridan family: The inspiration, support, and sacrifices you made have sustained me and made this work possible. It is your legacy too.

Contents

CONTENTS

Prologue

I BELIEVE WE are in a dark moment, perhaps one of the darkest in recent American history. The light at the end of the tunnel seems dim and distant most days. The current political landscape has left most good people, regardless of party affiliation or ideology, wondering *What can I do?* and *Can I make a difference?*

But there are flickers of light in the darkness, and they are growing, illuminating a path forward. These points of light come from us—the people of America who are answering the questions above with active and deliberate participation in the process that makes democracy powerful. Good can and does win, but it must get in the fight.

In the battles I have fought over the past three decades, when I've found myself losing, it was not because the opposition was better or their ideas were right—it was because good people were on the sidelines. Madeleine Albright's recent book, *Fascism: A Warning*, is a sober reminder that evil only wins when good abdicates.

I am an optimist by nature. I look at the moment we live

in now and hope that it is the darkness before the dawn. I can see elements of a new day in the November 2018 "blue wave" of more progressives, women, African Americans, Native Americans, Muslims, LGBT members in the House of Representatives. I see it in the unprecedented numbers of new voters registering, in the vigor of young people (shout-out to the Parkland kids), in the growing demands for a new political order, and in shifting demographics and political ideology.

My optimism arises in part because I'm assuming that if you've picked up this book, you want to help make the world a better place—and that's great, because the world needs you. Our country needs you. As the old saying goes, when there's a will, there's a way. I've learned this firsthand after spending my career as a public interest lobbyist tackling some of the most pernicious problems facing American society. Through many ups and downs and with the help of many partners and collaborators, I've seen great successes arise from some of society's biggest challenges—progress that wouldn't have happened without a problem to tackle and solve. In this book I want to share with you what I've learned about how brave efforts can and do create great leaps forward.

I, too, have been struggling since Election Day 2016 to find the right words to share and the right strategies to recommend. From crisis arises opportunity, and from the darkest moments shine forth the brightest lights. I know this because I have lived it. This is exactly the moment for the thinking, caring, compassionate "good people" and "better angels" among us, *including* us, to act. I hope the actions you read about in this book clearly show you that there is an answer to "What can I do?" In each story I tell in these chapters, a person just like you asked that question and answered it with actions that have changed the world for the better.

On the ground, each and every day, your work already helps make the nation a better place. You staff food pantries in church basements. You feed the hungry. You care for the sick. You cultivate boards to help achieve your mission. You raise funds, do outreach, organize events. You make America great. You may have been doing the good work for years now, or you may have just begun. Now, you have been presented with both an opportunity and the responsibility to be the glue that holds our nation together. Applying the lessons from this book helped pass vital social impact legislation in the past—and now, it can help you seize this moment.

Today's challenge, for the entire country, is to step up, lean in, push harder, and take action. Don't take the path of least resistance or, worse, stay silent in hopes of better times. Doing good requires more than just programs and services. It requires coordination, organization, and a new emphasis on and dedication to advocacy. Participating in advocacy is no longer a luxury—it is a necessity. Good can't happen if our government isn't forced to protect those who can't protect themselves. Good can't happen if there is no vision, no courage, and no strategy to make our voices heard in the halls of government.

I know that for many, budgets are tight and resources scarce. I also know some of you reading may have never done this type of work before. But when history recalls how

America recovered from this dark moment, I want it said that it was the people who stepped in and embodied our national motto, *e pluribus unum*—out of many, one. That it was the people who ensured that this remains the driving principle of America and ultimately the thing that retained and expanded her greatness.

When citizen activists have combined grassroots passion with smart political strategy, they have won some of the most transformative policy fights of our generation. In my experience these accomplishments come about when visionaries and activists team up with "white hat" lobbyists—people who understand the power of politics and who are able to put it to work to serve the public interest. For twenty-five years I've worked to master the art and science of winning for public interest causes. The culmination of that experience is presented here in a new theory for social change that I call the three P's. Successful campaigns and movements must possess a lobbyist's approach to *policy*, *politics*, and *press*; this is the formula for success. In my experience, leveraging the three P's, with true passion and discipline, can create results that are nothing short of awe-inspiring. At the end of each chapter I highlight some takeaway prescriptions for the reader, and there you can see how we applied the three P's for that particular issue.

In this book I offer lessons from the trenches on how some of this generation's most defining social issues—AIDS, disability rights, global poverty, cancer, human trafficking, national service, and social entrepreneurship—engendered landmark federal policies. I hope to inform, inspire, and entertain you, and to illustrate how we can apply a new formula for social change to create lasting impact, whether as engaged citizens, policy makers, supporters, or allies. More important, I want you to have an unvarnished view of the work, the required compromises, the personal tolls, the skills you develop after losing, the awesome power of democracy in action, and the sustaining effort to make change last.

Helping the Good Do Better pulls back the curtain on the corridors of power in Washington to reveal how social change really happens—from grassroots activism of ordinary citizens to presidential executive orders. This is not a textbook or a white paper. It's the story of my life's work and that of so many others—victims, culprits, constituents, representatives, allies, and opponents—who were at the table when policies were debated, tragedies suffered, and battles won. Each chapter tells the story of how a particular issue—often peripheral in society's eye at first—became legislation at the center of public debate, and with each one come valuable lessons on how we can win the battles we're fighting right now. Some efforts succeeded, and some failed, but each case provides powerful takeaways on how coalitions are built, political strategies crafted, and dominant interests challenged in high-stakes, no-holds-barred political battles. Some of the friends and colleagues who worked closely with me on these issues have provided their take. Throughout the book you'll see them giving a second view, providing their thoughts and perspectives on the stories I share.

Though the goals were different and the actors varied, I found a few things to be universal: even when a strong individual leader is present (and often one is required), every achievement is the result of collaboration. Building a strong coalition is intrinsic to success on a large scale. It requires symbiosis: each stakeholder has to recognize and understand how the partnership will benefit them and why they are a benefit to others. Second, winning requires strategy. Luck, good timing, and money all help, but an informed, strategic approach is required in order to achieve lasting effects.

People frequently act surprised when I tell them I'm a social worker. I think they assume all lobbyists are lawyers and that all social workers wear tunics and Birkenstocks. I get why folks are confused by my collection of power suits. But I'm proud of being both a social worker and a professional lobbyist—I believe my role is first and foremost that of advocate. My goals are to create change and solve human problems.

My very first job as a social worker set me on the path toward being a lobbyist. I was hired to open the first group home for developmentally disabled adults in my hometown. The first task was to request a zoning change—if you ever want to see raw, nasty political fights, go to a zoning board meeting. I'll save the details for later, but suffice it to say that things quickly got complicated, personal, and ugly. Soon my mom was driving ten more minutes over the state line to do her shopping in New Jersey rather than at the local grocery store so she wouldn't run into the neighbors and townspeople. That first experience said it all: there really is no change unless you do the hard work that comes with it.

No sooner had we gotten the group home open and

operating than the national political mood shifted with the election of Ronald Reagan to the White House (yes, elections have consequences). Suddenly and swiftly our entire budget supporting the home was threatened—cuts to every program for people with disabilities were proposed and passed within a year after the Reagan Revolution. That moment was my second fight—organizing every family member of our group home and all the staff and friends of staff I could muster. We raised hell and brought our issue directly to our congressman's office (he was a Republican). And we brought the press with us.

Our programs were spared, but the threats persisted. My fight to save the group home drew some attention, and I was offered a fellowship with the National Association of Social Workers in Washington, DC, and a chance to complete a master's degree at Catholic University of America in one year. I jumped at the opportunity, as I saw a path to more advocacy and greater impact. Not that my career proceeded smoothly from there. At the age of thirty, I borrowed $10,000 to venture out on my own, doff the aforementioned white hat, and found the Sheridan Group. I told my dad I would find enough work to pay him back within six months. I kept my promise.

When I started the Sheridan Group I was trying to take what I knew and share it with more than just one single-issue group at a time. The Sheridan Group's first client was the San Francisco AIDS Foundation, which donated a used fax machine to the "office"—a spare bedroom on the third floor of my townhouse.

A lot has changed in the twenty-five years since I founded the firm, but the goal has remained the same: to create effective strategies for socially responsible public policy initiatives. Our motto is "helping the good do better." Over the years, the Sheridan Group has become the go-to firm in the nation's capital for coalition-building and grassroots advocacy for nonprofits, social entrepreneurs, and other agents of change. I have spent my career using pragmatic politics to translate idealism into transformative public policy. It's not just about winning the fight, but about learning how to use all of the tools of policy, politics, and press to succeed in battle, again and again.

Jeanne White fought for and won an AIDS funding bill in the name of her dying son, Ryan; Bono and Jesse Helms came together to fight poverty in Africa; religious conservatives and liberal activists teamed up to pass the most important anti-trafficking bill of a generation—these scenes from twenty-five years in Washington fighting for the voiceless offer lessons about how Washington works, why politics matters, and how to win.

I hope you'll find these stories from the trenches to be funny, tragic, surprising, and memorable. But beyond spinning a good yarn, though I like to think I come by that skill honestly (thanks to my Irish roots), I hope you'll use these stories to apply the lessons in your own careers and pursuits in the public interest. And though you'll recognize some boldface names from pop culture, history, and politics, you'll also see that sometimes the best advice comes from the most unlikely advisors.

This is the updated battle plan for those who are ready to fight the good fight: social entrepreneurs, corporate CEOs, nonprofit managers, organizers, activists, philanthropists, and bloggers. We can all do our part to make government work *for* the people in order to create real and lasting change. Let's get down to business. There is more work to do.

CHAPTER 1

AIDS and the Ryan White CARE Act

"If it's good enough for Mother Teresa, it's good enough for you"

APRIL 24, 1990. The world had just watched a boy die, one of the most impassioned advocates of his generation. Ryan White had just died of AIDS, and I was in the midst of a desperate battle to pass a bill that would provide care to others who were suffering from the disease. I had invited Ryan's mother, Jeanne, to Washington to help me gather support for the bill, and we hit the halls of Capitol Hill.

We needed to add fourteen senators as co-sponsors in order to get to the needed number of sixty so that Senator Jesse Helms, the homophobic arch-right-wing senior senator from North Carolina, wouldn't be able to filibuster. One of our main targets for the day was Senator Joe Biden. When he came out of the Senate chamber he looked hurried, clearly in no mood for chitchat. But I ran up and quickly got in a word. Ryan White's mother had just flown in the night before. She was standing right behind me, and she wanted to speak to him. He stopped in his tracks and immediately took her hand. This act of intimacy took Jeanne and me both by surprise. Joe Biden is, in many ways, the quintessential charismatic politician, yet he, too, has suffered a great loss. In 1972—as he prepared to be sworn in as a senator—Biden's wife and daughter were killed in a car accident on the way home from picking out the family Christmas tree. His two sons barely survived, and Biden nursed them back to full recovery as a single father.

As I stood nearby, I heard Jeanne start her request for Biden's support. He stopped her midsentence. "You don't need to tell me the pain of losing a child," he told her. "I have been there, and there is nothing more painful a parent can experience." They both started to cry. Hell, even *I* started to cry. The world around us came to a complete stop. Senators came in and out, staff bustled around, but a protective bubble seemed to envelop us. Something magical was happening.

By the end of his deeply personal conversation with Jeanne, I knew that the power of Biden's and Jeanne's shared passion, grief, and hope would be an unstoppable force if it could be harnessed on behalf of all the parents and families who had lost someone to AIDS. There is a strange peace and deep authenticity that comes with such pain—as if there is little else in the world that can hurt so much and, thus, nothing in the world left to fear.

Grief is a powerful force, and it animated the AIDS movement. If turned inward, grief can destroy lives and create further suffering. If turned outward, however, it can heal the deepest wounds, bring together fierce enemies, and birth what some might call miracles. Perhaps that is why the height of the AIDS epidemic, which is where this story begins, was at once so tragic and so miraculous. AIDS brought fear, shame, anger, and division to this country as it arbitrarily stole friends, family members, and colleagues. Yet, AIDS created a shared suffering. It cut across race, creed, socioeconomic status, and sexual orientation and introduced a degree of compassion and humility that few could have predicted. In this sense, AIDS was the great leveler of our time. Our response—as individuals and as a country—was a test of our common humanity. This chapter tells the story of how we fared in that test, what we learned, and how these lessons may help us address the challenges ahead.

In 1984, a thirteen-year-old hemophiliac contracted a mystifying illness from a contaminated blood treatment. Ryan White was, like most people diagnosed with AIDS, given six months or less to live—it was a death sentence. Back in his hometown in Indiana, he tried to return to school but faced enormous opposition: beyond taunts, threats, and abuse, parents and teachers organized and rallied to prevent him from attending school. At the time, there were fewer than 150 cases of pediatric AIDS in the country, and being diagnosed with the disease carried an enormous social stigma. But Ryan was undeterred. He and his family fought back against the school. As Ryan's case gained attention, celebrities like Elton

3

John, Michael Jackson, and Phil Donahue took up support of his legal battle. Along the way Ryan White became a national celebrity and advocate for AIDS education and research. AIDS in the 1980s was a wholly different disease than the one we know today; it was not chronically managed, widely understood, or accepted. It was lethal, highly stigmatized, and characterized by a national mood of crisis, desperation, anger, and scornful discrimination.

In 1984, I was twenty-four years old, making a whopping $15 a day working for Walter Mondale on his quest to deny Ronald Reagan a second term. I had a newly minted master's degree in social work and, to my parents' regret, was spending my life as a political organizer and vagabond. (A quick note for new and young change makers: when you first start out, money probably won't be a priority, and your loved ones will likely think you are nuts.) I was actually in Ryan's home state of Indiana working on the primary when his story broke. I remember the campaign briefly discussing this issue but clearly sidelining it for its "controversy." My focus then was winning the Indiana primary and moving on to the other states we needed to win to claim the nomination in San Francisco that summer. I had a front seat for the history-making moment when Geraldine Ferraro became the first woman to be nominated for vice president by a major party, and then we got crushed. After a few months of looking for work, I landed happily at the Child Welfare League of America as deputy director.

Those years were among the most dramatic and formulating in my life. My job at CWLA involved work on membership campaigns, conferences, and public policy. Essentially anything that interested me or needed to be done, I got a chance to do. I was immediately drawn to a policy agenda that centered on children with disabilities thanks to my experience in my first job as a social worker, when I worked on similar issues. Disability groups were not only working on disability policy but also rapidly taking their cause to the civil rights agenda, so I was able to network and grow my contacts in diverse contexts and on diverse causes, including AIDS.

This was also the time in my life when I met my husband, Vincent Walsh. It was a chance meeting at a bar in Dupont Circle and, since I was leaving on a trip the next day, we agreed to meet up when I returned. We still don't agree about the occasion of that first date—I say it was for lunch, Vince says for dinner, but we were married on June 21, 2014—almost twenty-eight years to the day after we first met. Coming to grips with my homosexuality was complicated. On top of all the obvious issues an Irish Catholic kid from New York would have in coming out, I added a level of complexity to it by choosing politics—and perhaps elective office someday—as a career goal. In 1986, being an openly gay man was almost certainly a career-ending declaration for someone who wanted to run for office. I did eventually come out, first to my siblings and then, a few years later, to my parents, but during this time in my life I remained publicly closeted.

Early on in my time at CWLA we were asked to lend policy and political support to create a highly specialized foster care program to care for orphaned AIDS children—

the "boarder babies." In most cases the mothers did not know they were HIV-positive, so the "death sentence" for both mother and infant came simultaneously. These babies spent all of their short lives in hospital nurseries because they lacked foster parents who were sensitized to the special needs of AIDS infants, and many families looking to adopt were afraid to take them in. The stigma of AIDS was powerful and isolating.

Before I knew it, I headed to the Hill to find support, and soon we were drafting legislation and creating a strategy to pass it. We didn't know it then, but this bill would soon become the first positive piece of AIDS legislation to win federal support—the Abandoned Infants Assistance Act of 1988. It was a rather simple bill, just an additional amount of money state foster care agencies could use to train, support, and recruit specialized foster parents caring for children born with the HIV virus. We consciously decided to tuck this little bill into a much bigger bill where it was carried through the legislative process relatively unnoticed. Democratic senator Howard Metzenbaum from Ohio was the sponsor and Senator Edward M. (Ted) Kennedy from Massachusetts was the committee chairman who guided its passage. It was the beginning of an incredible and nearly totally accidental journey that became a major defining chapter in my life.

During my time at CWLA I was approached by the leaders of AIDS Action Council, an association of six AIDS service organizations (ASOs). AIDS Action had been created in 1984 to work with Congress and the administration to bring the voices of the ASOs to the policy table. They had seen the work I'd done on the Abandoned Infants Act and offered me a job as executive director. I declined for a variety of reasons; at the time I was only out to my closest friends, and taking on AIDS seemed like it would be too revealing and too political. I also didn't think an executive director job was right for me—I didn't want the hassle of budgets and boards. I did mention a few colleagues who I thought would be better for the job, including Jean McGuire, a friend of mine who had worked with me on disabilities. Shortly afterward I received a call from Jean; she was grateful for the recommendation, but would only take the job if I agreed to be her policy director.

Jean was someone I could count on, someone who could make this adventure tolerable—if not thrilling. And the need for more legislative pressure regarding AIDS was appallingly obvious. Still, I wasn't sure how public I wanted to be about my involvement in AIDS activism. I was thinking of running for Congress in New York in a few years—and a young gay man working on AIDS legislation was bound to attract certain labels that could be major obstacles on such a career path.

So, I did what any conflicted Irishman would do—I asked my grandmother. After Easter dinner, I took her aside and explained my trepidation. To my surprise, she said simply, "Thomas, if working on AIDS is good enough for Mother Teresa, then it's good enough for you." I began at AIDS Action as director of policy and government affairs in 1988.

An idealistic twenty-something, I had no idea what I was getting into. I may have had an ounce of Mother Teresa's passion for helping the suffering, but I lacked her patience and beatific attitude completely, that's for sure.

———

When I first joined AIDS Action there had been little federal policy for the AIDS community to celebrate. We didn't have time to waste. Ryan White and hundreds of thousands of others were getting sicker, slipping toward death every day. But in the meantime, they were living, and fighting, and taking a stand: Ryan was featured on the cover of *People* magazine, was brought onstage by Elton John at a fundraiser and got his first car, a Chevrolet Cavalier given by the Indiana Independent Auto Dealers Association.

AIDS Action had an official public policy committee, but in reality, real-time decisions were made by just three people: me; Pat Christen, the executive director of the San Francisco AIDS Foundation; and Tim Sweeney of Gay Men's Health Crisis in New York. A graduate of Stanford's pre-med program, Pat had just returned from two years with the Peace Corps in Africa when we met at an AIDS public policy roundtable in Washington in spring 1988. At twenty-seven, she was tall, blond, strikingly beautiful, and wicked smart, as they'd say in Boston. Pat started out as a volunteer on the crisis switchboard at SFAF and became the organization's public policy director and then its executive director in less than three years' time. AIDS accelerated calendars and careers. Tim Sweeney was an Irish Catholic like me, with a short, slight build and a much larger personality. When we were in financial straits, Tim was able to raise money from the wealthy New York gay community faster than anyone else I knew. His loyalty and influence were incredibly helpful during the most stressful moments.

At the outset of this work Pat, Tim, Jean, and I discovered that there was little, if any, strategic thinking, political capital, or sophisticated organizing present in the AIDS community for policy. A note on political capital: if you are trying to rally interest, support or money for a cause, stop and ask yourself, *Why does anyone with political power care about your issues? Do you donate money to their campaigns or interests? Do you organize voters? Are you popular with the press?* Political capital is a standard that measures your relevance in the political circles that decide policy matters. Substance matters, but politics drives priorities and decisions regarding what gets done and what gets left behind. Like money, you earn political capital the hard way, you invest it wisely, and you are very careful how you spend it. It is very easy to go "bankrupt" on social issues and causes if you spend your political capital too freely or blow it all at once.

In the AIDS community, there were inspiring acts of local action and demonstrations of courage and compassion that I have rarely witnessed since. I went to my first AIDS Walk in Atlanta at the invitation of AID Atlanta's executive director Sandy Thurman. She was especially keen for me to see the display of support from all walks of life in a city like Atlanta. She understood the political power of that—and it was a stunning display of community diversity and caring (even in the South) at a time when that was rare. My tour of the AIDS ward at San Francisco General Hospital was to this day the most compassionate health care environment I've ever seen—doctors, nurses, volunteers, patients, friends, and family members were all in—one unit of love and care. It was a war zone by every standard I can imagine, but the cohesion is what I remember most. My purpose for going to SFGH that day was to see firsthand what the San Francisco model was in terms of communities responding to the raging epidemic. The SF model was the starting point in what was to become the Ryan White CARE Act, and this tour on that day was the beginning of my understanding of services that needed to be supported in a policy initiative that actually would work. Ground-up knowledge and perspective remain the cornerstone of good policy and the hallmark of policy that actually implements well in the end.

There wasn't a lack of great work and compassionate support in the nation at this moment; it was there in pockets like Atlanta and San Francisco. What we were lacking was a national funnel through which real change and solutions could be optimized. We needed to build our political capital, as we had no currency in the political marketplace, and there was no reason yet for anyone on Capitol Hill to care about our issues. On top of that, we were acting on behalf of a group of people—largely IV drug users and homosexuals—who were at the absolute bottom of the constituency rankings. Most members were not only unresponsive to such voters but would practically run the other direction at their mention.

We soon discovered we also had deep divisions within the AIDS community to contend with, most fiercely related to three issues: public health versus civil rights, research versus prevention and care, and integrated versus segregated AIDS services.

The first dividing line concerned whether to make the case for AIDS funding through a strictly public health system lens or to portray it more through a civil rights lens. The gay community saw AIDS as a potential precursor to and justification for a more robust gay civil rights agenda. But the public health crisis gave us our strongest case for federal intervention. If we could carefully shape our messaging so that it wasn't seen as a vote for or against the gay community, we would be able to create a larger framework of support. Thus, my first and most difficult task was to shift the entire political paradigm of the AIDS debate.

Another fierce debate in the AIDS community was whether to focus on research for drugs to cure or slow HIV in order to care for those who were probably going to die anyway, or to focus on prevention efforts to stop new infections. Some members of the AIDS community really wanted to prioritize prevention, but we just didn't have the political capital at the time. Politically, we couldn't talk about sex education, condoms, gay relationships, needle exchange—nothing! Others thought that since the real goal was finding a cure, everything else should fall to the wayside. From our viewpoint, however, there was only one clear priority: care. AIDS was dooming individuals and families to poverty. We had to start getting resources to those who didn't have the option to pay for care or treatment themselves. The view that anything less than a cure was a distraction struck me as classically elitist, but moreover it was useless in the political or policy realm.

Among those who agreed that care was the priority for federal policy efforts, there was another heated debate: What setting could best offer services for AIDS patients? Many at the time were pressing for a totally separate system of services for the AIDS community, including separate hospitals and community clinics. This notion of a separate system really bothered me. I believed we had to move the issue back to the broader public health system debate with a much more holistic view. In the end, we believed our efforts on AIDS were merely bridges to a time when the nation would improve its overall health care system, particularly for people with disabilities and diseases.

In retrospect, I probably wasn't as mindful as I should have been about the real bitterness and anger that our approach caused among some members of the AIDS community, and I regret not finding more diplomatic ways to reach a consensus on these issues. I burned some bridges and lost some friends in the fight, but I knew when I embarked on the work that there might be a price to pay. Looking deeper and more personally, being closeted at the time may have been a latent reason for my quest to push the issue away from a "gay agenda," but the political realities were undeniable as well. I was frequently the only one in the room who had ever worked in electoral politics. That made me an outlier and sometimes a pariah with my nonprofit colleagues.

What's more, I did understand that for the gay community in the late eighties the link between AIDS and civil rights was strong and directly causal. But linking them in an effort to confront a public health epidemic was a losing strategy. For me it came down to a choice—run the strategy through public health policy portals or through the lens of civil rights. The decision to go public health was the correct one, but at that time, veering from civil rights felt like one more betrayal and one more setback to the gay community. I understood the anger, resentment, and frustration, and I paid the price of a few personal friendships lost or never formed, and in a few cases a permanent dislike. So be it. There is a price for this work and these roles. Let me be the first to tell you: no one should set out to be a change maker without understanding the price you may be asked to pay.

If we had had the luxury of time, I could have spent more of it debating options and crafting compromises, but a ticking clock in 1989 was a death sentence for so many. We had made our decisions, and now it was time to get down to work.

———

At that point, Congress's only actions had been simply allocating more money for AIDS research at the National Institutes of Health, and giving the Centers for Disease Control funding to collect AIDS statistics and disseminate limited information to the public. Then suddenly Jesse Helms taught us the hard way what happens when the right kind of political pressure is absent. He started introducing amendments in every health appropriations bill to prevent funding for prevention education that might in any way condone homosexual behavior. It became practically an annual tradition—the appropriations bill for health-related spending would come up, and Helms would offer what we called his "no promo homo" clause. Within my first month on the job at AIDS Action, I had my first humiliating encounter with Helms, when he introduced this amendment to the annual appropriations bill in 1988.

It was my first time at the tiller leading AIDS Action's efforts. We had the beginnings of a coalition, but we were a very small band of advocates against a very savvy and skilled senator, one who terrorized his colleagues by concocting amendments with so much ugliness that a recorded vote would create a political crisis. Once a vote was required, members needed to say yea or nay publicly—on the record. Votes framed as promoting homosexuality or condoning pornography as Helms framed it were surely going to be turned into thirty-second TV ads at election time. Remember the Willie Horton ad used against Michael Dukakis? He was a murderer who committed another murder after being furloughed from jail through a program created by Dukakis. Those kinds of ads are coin of the realm for right-wing attack campaigns, and sadly, they are usually effective. The bottom line for us was that Helms was using the vote to bring a world of trouble to a senator supporting AIDS issues during reelection. On the night before the appropriations bill, as we gathered in the Senate anteroom, prepared with briefing books, talking points, data, and support letters from major medical and public health groups, six of us waited for the inevitable news of an attack by Helms. Senator Kennedy and his staff came out from the Senate cloakroom and reported that Helms had brought explicit comic books and was showing videos of proper condom use produced by Gay Men's Health Crisis in New York. The comic books were erotic, and the video was explicit, by design. Condoms and safe sex were the only defense against the raging virus, and Helms was attacking at the core of that strategy. Kennedy was clear that the message in the cloakroom of the US Senate was "If you don't vote for the Helms amendment, these comic books and videos will find their way to your constituents via Helms's political action committee, and you'll be toast." You see, Jesse Helms didn't just play dirty on the Senate floor (or show "dirty" comics in the cloakroom); he backed up his bigotry with millions of dollars from a political action committee that was used brutally against Republicans and Democrats alike in close elections. His millions came from donations mostly from evangelical Christians. Whether we were ready or not, we were now playing hardball in the big leagues.

Thankfully, we had a heavy hitter on our team: Senator Ted Kennedy had emerged as a leading AIDS advocate. I first met Senator Kennedy when I was working for the Child Welfare League. He was, of course, the lion of the Senate, but he also chaired the powerful Health, Education, Labor, and Pensions (HELP) Committee in the Senate. All our issues at the Child Welfare League went through his committee, and my job required me to work with Kennedy and his staff on a regular basis. In May 1987, he introduced the AIDS Federal Policy Act (S. 1220), which sought to provide funding for testing, counseling, research, and patient access to experimental drugs. It passed the Senate, but similar House bills that year didn't fare as well. Despite herculean efforts by many tireless people, at that moment we couldn't see much progress. Yet these early defeats taught us to do our homework and forced us to rework the content and language of the bills, in order to be better prepared for next time.

Ever so slowly, we could sense something start to shift. A small number of legislators—like Representative Nancy Pelosi (D-CA), Representative Henry Waxman (D-CA), Representative Barbara Boxer (D-CA), Representative Ted Weiss (D-NY), and Senator Alan Cranston (D-CA), whose districts were facing major public health disasters, were becoming more powerful advocates. But there was a bigger reason why 1988 was a tipping point when momentum behind the AIDS crisis quickly gathered speed: the epidemic had become much more widespread. Sadly, it was only after the death toll mounted that more and more family members and friends joined us in demanding a more effective and compassionate response to the AIDS crisis. It was during this time that AIDS began to touch my life personally; my partner, Vince, had an ex-boyfriend who suddenly became ill, an alumnus from our Mondale campaign team died, and another dear friend, unable to even tell us he had AIDS, stayed with us as he got sicker and sicker.

As painful as these deaths were, the stories of desperation and anger of hundreds of thousands of Americans (not just gay men) who were being affected by this epidemic created a powerful chorus. Stories were voiced by more and more people, at an increasing volume. These were the voices that needed to be heard on Capitol Hill. These were the people who would finally silence Helms. And so, for the next two years, we went to work on giving them the biggest amplifier we could find—it was time to truly do battle.

———

To mount this battle, we knew we'd need an army. Jean and I were part of an informal network called the Second Monday Group. There were about six of us, all working in different areas of the AIDS field. We met once a month to discuss policy strategy, usually at the cozy Tabard Inn restaurant in Dupont Circle. One evening, in a burst of frustration, I said, "Look, if we continue to keep this to just a conversation between ourselves, we're never gonna get anywhere. We need bigger players, and we need to invite them in."

Shortly afterward we devised core operating principles for a much larger, more serious organization. We called it NORA—National Organizations Responding to AIDS. The strategy was simple: we needed the major players from the associations that had the most to win or lose from AIDS policy decisions to get on board. We knew winning was about numbers, names, and credibility—we needed to build a big tent, get as many people inside it as possible, and then get meaningful contributions from all of them. We went after the idea with a vengeance. The structure of this coalition, its operating principles and procedures, and its capacity to carry a complex and comprehensive agenda were unprecedented in public health history.

Eventually we had a diverse and eclectic group of more than one hundred members, including the American Hospital Association, the American Medical Association, the American Nurses Association, and the American Public Health Association. We also had a variety of smaller groups, and even some surprising members, like the US Conference of Catholic Bishops. Sharon Daley, their lobbyist, told us she "couldn't touch prevention," because that meant condom distribution and sex education, and "probably not civil rights either," because that meant talking about gays and lesbians. But she could get to nuns and priests who were working in hospices and caring for AIDS victims all over the country. It was evident that different organizations were coming to the table to accomplish or promote very different things, but we were fine with that, so long as everyone participated in some way. We began holding monthly meetings around an ambitious agenda: care, prevention, research, pediatrics, and civil rights. Each of these issues had its own task force, and while one of my major roles was chairing the care task force, I was also working hard to keep the entire coalition together.

Running and managing a large coalition of divergent vested interests is tough. Doing so in the middle of a virtual hurricane of politics swirling around what had become a pandemic made it feel like madness every hour of every day. To maintain calm, stay on strategy, and enforce cohesion, I lost any hope of winning the Miss Congeniality sash.

There were hurt feelings, squashed egos, bitter fights, and I'm sure long-term resentments. I had some bad moments, including threatening a lobbyist who was double-dealing for his own organization's favor outside of the coalition's strict rules. "Dave" was the chief lobbyist for a national network of health centers, and he and his organization were important to our effort to push AIDS care into the mainstream public health systems, but he couldn't help himself from wanting a bit more for his group by cutting out others. Privately I got word that he was shopping an amendment to the bill we were all pushing in order to create an exclusive funding stream just for his constituency. When I was told of this effort, I hit the roof. A cardinal rule of good coalitions is "all for one and one for all," and he'd just betrayed it. I called him up and asked him to see me in Kennedy's Senate health committee offices that day. When he walked in there were three or four people in our mini war room in Hart 527. I stood and quietly walked up to him and got close, very close, in-your-face close. I pressed my finger into his chest and simply said in a quiet, firm voice: "One more conversation about an amendment to anyone and your entire provision will be stuck from the bill. You'll be out, and I'll tell your board exactly why it happened." He got in line and never wandered again, but I imagine it left a bad impression. In those moments I always hoped I'd smooth things over after success had been achieved. But the goal of the moment was more important. We began to win fights and advance our agenda. Slowly but surely, amid the chaos progress was visible.

The first real order of business for NORA was passing Kennedy's S. 1220 bill, which sought to do no less than increase staff at the Centers for Disease Control; create a national AIDS research program; engage in greater international outreach; fund informational programs on AIDS at the federal, state, and local levels; provide training programs for health care workers; and establish care and treatment programs for AIDS victims. The bill was also a bit of a straw man. We wanted to see what we could get away with—to test the waters for a bigger bill down the line. We knew we had to start getting into the front of the debate rather than countering Helms's amendments. Then, from out of nowhere, a mighty gift was dropped in our lap. In the summer of 1988, Michael Iskowitz joined our ranks as the health policy fellow in Kennedy's office, and with him came an entirely new energy, intellect, and larger-than-life flamboyance.

Michael was wicked smart; he ate, slept, and breathed the AIDS cause and worked around the clock. After preparing until two in the morning for a hearing the next day, he would think of some obscure argument that the opposition might throw at us, like the possibility of tsetse flies migrating across the Atlantic on African fishing vessels. It drove us crazy at times. But his command of these details made it readily apparent why Kennedy, as well as straitlaced Republicans like Orrin Hatch, loved and trusted him so much.

By the winter of 1989, I had pretty much moved into Michael's office. We spent at least eighteen hours a day together—most of them negotiating bill provisions on the phone with the congressional staff and NORA members. We ate three meals a day of disgusting Senate cafeteria food, usually consisting of limp french fries and overripe melon. It was a unique relationship between an advocate and a Hill staffer, the likes of which would be hard to find today. We were a real team. To this day I keep Michael in mind as I work with Hill staff. They may be young and inexperienced, but hard work, clear motives, and unflinching focus on details create an environment for powerful members to do mighty and historic things. Senator Kennedy was our champion, but Michael was the muscle. In fact, I've asked Michael to be the second view on this issue, so you will hear more from him at the end of this chapter.

One of the reasons Michael was so dedicated to the cause was the experience of losing his mentor Terry Beirn. Terry had been assigned by the American Foundation for AIDS Research (AMFAR) to Kennedy's office about a year before Michael arrived, and they soon became best friends. Terry operated at a feverish pitch—despite his failing health due to AIDS. He made his mark mentoring Michael and moving a progressive, thoughtful public policy agenda forward, and he died knowing the bill was on a trajectory to pass. Though he didn't live to see it signed into law, the NIH provision of S. 1220 is named the Terry Beirn Research Initiative.

Compared to my relationship with Michael and Terry on the Senate side, the one I enjoyed with Tim Westmoreland, Waxman's head legislative aid for health issues, was not as close. Yet Tim was just as critical as Michael in helping to move CARE on the House side. For those who may not recall high school civics, the House and Senate are independent bodies of our Congress. They can and do write vastly different versions of bills, even on the same exact topic. The House and Senate have their own committee structures, and as a result the substance, jurisdiction, and politics of each chamber's deliberations can produce divergent results. The process is complicated. Usually a bill begins its path to passage at a subcommittee level, progresses to the full committee, and finally makes its way onto the House or Senate floor. Stop for a moment and count here—that is six different times in a process where help or harm can come to a bill trying to become a law. This represents both the fundamental opportunity in working in legislative advocacy and the existential threat that you face on the way to progress and change. In the end it is the promise of democracy at work, but it isn't easy. *Schoolhouse Rock* had a brilliant little ditty on this process called "I'm Just a Bill." It was a rhyming musical tutorial on how a bill becomes a law, and it's still one of my favorite things to cite (and occasionally sing) for audiences when I do lobby training 101. Winning a perfect bill on one side can easily be matched with a very bad or even no bill on the other. The trick is to get two similar bills moving through both chambers at the same time so you can at some point produce a bill that both chambers agree to pass onto the president for signature. In this case, the House was a more challenging chamber for us than the Senate.

Tim was more personally conservative and cerebral; his complete mastery of the data and issues surrounding US health care policy, especially around AIDS, was nearly en-cyclopedic. With Michael and Tim's help, we put together an insider's strategy of developing champions and friends in the House and Senate—one member at a time. Then we at NORA brought them concepts to appeal to individual inter-ests, and we went from there. We had provisions to help hos-pitals, doctors, and nurses; we included social workers and volunteers; we gave power to community groups and some control to mayors. It was a privilege to have had so many talented people bringing ideas and expertise to the process. When people talk about "the infamous AIDS lobby," this is the feature I think they should envy most. All good lobbies have insiders and outsiders. The insiders are the champions on the Hill; the outsiders are those not in the halls of Con-gress but rather in the trenches of "real life," able to offer ideas and most importantly apply pressure when needed. In this case the outsiders were the members of AIDS Action and those 120 representatives of NORA who gave us their ideas and resources and the power of collective action.

All our hard work paid off on November 4, 1988, when President Reagan signed Kennedy's S. 1220 and the larger S. 2889, the Health Omnibus Programs Extension (HOPE) bill, including Title II Programs with Respect to Acquired Immune Deficiency Syndrome, into law. The final bill cer-tainly wasn't perfect—like all things in politics, it was a compromise. But it was *something*. That January, we held a party in the Senate Labor Committee's hearing room in memory of Terry and to celebrate all the good that he—and so many others who had also departed—had accomplished in passing the HOPE provisions. It was a bittersweet occasion. A more comprehensive and compassionate federal AIDS response was still needed, and the battle was rapidly approaching. It was sure to be an ugly fight.

As 1989 dawned, NORA refined its efforts to focus on three measurable goals. First, win appropriations for AIDS research. Second, pass civil rights legislation under the Americans with Disabilities Act. And third, expedite the FDA's process for approving experimental AIDS drugs. 1989 also marked the beginning of a new Congress (the 101st) and a new administration under President George H. W. Bush. In December 1988, the NORA leadership arrived early to a large conference room in the transition team's offices in DC. The doors finally swung open, and in walked the president-elect. We were shocked—we had not expected to see him in person; we had prepared to meet with some of his staff. We gathered ourselves and made our pitch. He listened intently and then pledged to "do better on this issue." The bizarre moment seemed to offer a glimmer of hope toward opening a dialogue.

But contrary to his pledge to do better, Bush allotted no new money for AIDS in his proposed fiscal year 1990 budget. This was largely a continuation of Reagan's policy of avoiding AIDS, but it also perpetuated the previous eight years of slashing and burning the domestic budget. The budget and appropriations process in this kind of environment was going to be brutal. All the AIDS bills in the world wouldn't mean anything if they never got funded. There was also growing concern by other health groups that we (the AIDS lobby) were going to take some of their funding—especially at the NIH.

At the suggestion of Congresswoman Barbara Boxer, we connected with the newly appointed Representative Nancy Pelosi; Pelosi was initially appointed to her seat after the death of Congresswoman Sala Burton. This was an issue that was incredibly important to Pelosi; in her opening remarks after being appointed to the House she mentioned the AIDS epidemic and her intention to seek a solution to the crisis during her time in the House. To Pelosi this seemed like an obvious goal, but her colleagues scolded her for bringing controversy to the floor. Thankfully, she never let that stop her and became a huge champion for the issue. From that first moment to this very moment as I write these words, Nancy Pelosi remains a champion. She was there in the early and somewhat darker days, she was there as we gained political capital and began winning, and she led the way when AIDS went global. When she became Speaker of the House the entire domestic and international health agenda got action and, more important, urgently needed resources. She'll appear again and again in this book because she has tirelessly worked her way into the history of so many issues. It was an accident of history that I've had this long and privileged relationship with her for nearly thirty years.

With the support of Boxer and Pelosi we decided to ask Representative Leon Panetta, the powerful chair of the

House Budget Committee, to hold budget hearings on AIDS funding. Boxer was a member of the committee, and her California colleague Panetta was chair. When we told her of our intent to approach Panetta, she loved the idea. She, Pelosi, and Panetta took the same flight every week back and forth to SFO, and the two women decided they'd work on Panetta personally on the plane. Panetta didn't agree the first time we asked, but when he got on the plane to go home, he had two seatmates who made the final and successful push. The following Tuesday when they all returned to DC, we got an okay to hold the hearing at the full committee level—Panetta would chair it himself. Sometimes the first ask is the hardest, but we knew that we had support within that committee and we hoped this would get the issue the attention it needed. Budgets are really just advisory; they don't have the power of law, but they do set the tone and the priority list for the actual spending bills. This was an enormous opportunity because it allowed us to show a list of all past authorizations, budget requests, and actual appropriations (or lack thereof) for all AIDS-related items. Using these baseline figures, we could then provide justifications and recommendations for future funding. We worked the budget process hard that winter and spring and, by the time we had finished, had built a solid case for our funding requests, all vetted in public hearings and on the record.

This single strategy was, as we began to learn, the cornerstone of a fast and effective AIDS budget and appropriations strategy. It was a strategy born not out of any terrific brilliance but simply out of the need to go where we could win. Boxer's district included San Francisco, so she was a fierce champion on the AIDS issue. She was also part of a very close delegation of Bay Area representatives that included Leon Panetta and Nancy Pelosi. Boxer's willingness to press Panetta to chair these hearings was the main reason we pursued this avenue. Frankly, we didn't have many other cards to play.

By October of that year we had seen our first major victories: a doubling in NIH funding that fiscal year, S. 1220 became law, new bureaucratic policy levers around NIH were going to be put in place, and we were negotiating aggressively with the FDA on expediting approval of experimental drugs. We also had made a good start on the Americans with Disabilities Act (which we hoped would subsume all civil rights–related issues pertaining to AIDS), and were ready to move on to the next big challenge.

We soon started to realize that we couldn't just keep funding research. We had to get out of the "white coats and stethoscope" mode—which was the only safe place to be politically—and start helping the organizations trying to care for people with AIDS. The practical measure of successful public policy is always public benefit, and that was singularly missing from the AIDS policy debate up until that moment. Thus, we began a conversation with a small group of AIDS policy experts. One of the first recommendations from these discussions was that we take on entitlement reform—that is, we should make Medicare and Medicaid more accessible for AIDS patients so they would not have to wait twenty-four months to be considered "disabled" to qualify for Medicare or to spend down all their money to poverty levels to qualify for Medicaid.

Prevention was a trickier matter because it meant talking about condoms and homosexuality and drug abuse. Any attempt at a serious and meaningful prevention strategy was sure to bring Helms and company to the party. We knew an all-out confrontation over AIDS prevention was unlikely to be winnable. Practicalities are not always easy to embrace, especially when shelving a critical element of your public health strategy will result in more people infected with HIV. But, in the final analysis, care offered our best and possibly only chance to win.

Part of the process we used to reach this conclusion was a strategic meeting with key members of Congress and their senior staff. When I would discuss the matter with Orrin Hatch, he told me frankly that he couldn't support us on most of the prevention issues but that he "did care about how these people [AIDS patients] were treated—especially in their final days." This sort of "care for sinner without condoning the sin" philosophy was fairly typical of Christian conservatives, who were at their apex of power at the time.

I started to realize that we could win over these pragmatic and more compassionate conservatives like Orrin Hatch (as well as the fiscal conservatives who hated entitlement programs) if we could create a cost-effective model that relied on early intervention and outpatient/community/home-based care, one that could act as a bridge from work to disability. If we could get conservatives to come to our side strictly on the merits of public health and fiscal arguments, then this could really be the next frontier for a major AIDS bill. However, first we had to know what was really needed in terms of care on the front lines.

———

In the fall of 1989, Ryan White appeared on the cover of *Life* magazine for a special issue about stories that defined the decade. Around the same time, eight of us from AIDS Action gathered in San Francisco for an informal policy brainstorming meeting. Pat Christen agreed to host us, and we were joined by Tim Sweeney, Glen Maxey (head of the Austin AIDS Project and later to become the first openly gay elected official in Texas), Don Schmidt from the New Mexico AIDS Project, John Mortimore of AIDS Project LA, Mike Richards from Houston, and Larry Kessler from Boston.

At the beginning of the first day, I asked the group: "What could the federal government do to help you do your jobs better every day?" Their answers were simple: create more political leverage, especially with city officials who controlled public health systems and access to care; provide access to more resources, especially case management; and clear away bureaucracy. Next, we needed a central argument that would have the power to move legislators to our side. And this is where Pat Christen offered an incredibly powerful idea—one that framed the problem in crystal-clear terms.

Our meeting took place just two weeks after Hurricane Hugo devastated much of coastal South Carolina. The country, Pat pointed out, responded to the crisis with an all-out effort. "Why," demanded Pat, "does the federal government have the ability to shift resources to deal with a hurricane or an earthquake, but can't seem to move a finger to come to the rescue of our public health infrastructure? AIDS is destroying it nearly as much as an unexpected weather occurrence." The concept of "disaster/emergency relief" was born in this moment and prevailed as a central message of our legislative and communications strategy throughout.

But during these deliberations our brilliant and lofty moments were balanced with some raw political calculus, too. As we worked our way into details for the bill's outline, we needed to decide which cities in America had the emergency and needed disaster assistance. We pulled out the CDC's document that chronicled the number of people who had been diagnosed and had died in each city and state in the United States and its territories. We scrolled through—at 20,000 cases we had five cities; at 15,000 cases we had eight cities; at 10,000 cases we had ten cities. I stopped the morbid roll call and simply asked, "Where is Boston, Massachusetts?" "It's number ten at just over 10,000 cases," came the answer from Tim Sweeney. "We can stop there," I said. "Senator Kennedy will be our champion, and we aren't going to bring him this bill unless I can tell him we will be sure AIDS in Massachusetts is being addressed." And that is exactly what the original outline of the bill had as its marker—ten cities at 10,000 cases or more. Over the years I've actually been in rooms where bureaucrats, academics, and even latter-day advocates have waxed on and on about the deep and thoughtful analysis that constituted the development of that formula, and I've always wanted to stand up and say, "BS." I never have, but for this moment—and for history—this is the simple truth from the guy who was in the room where it happened.

By the time we finished our meeting we had a conceptual framework for the bill and had also hammered out some of the more practical concerns. The federal government needed to provide emergency assistance to the hardest-hit cities, support statewide planning in service delivery, ensure continuation of insurance for people with AIDS, leverage the power of local governments and community-based organizations, and give everyone a seat at the table (including AIDS patients themselves) when it came to setting priorities for the use of funds.

Perhaps the most powerful and unique feature of our bill, however, was the degree of local control that it gave constituents when it came to spending federal dollars. This was a major talking point of Republicans at the time, and making it a central theme of our new model allowed us to expand our support in Congress and also allowed the bill to work effectively and quickly. As a condition for receiving funding, every grantee had to establish a planning council. This was our way of making sure that cities invested the money in priority areas according to the priorities set by people with AIDS and those responsible for serving them, not according to political favors and whims. The whole design was about getting states and cities to kick in money, and giving power to the stakeholders. Getting away from orthodoxy—being willing to see another's view and then interpret it for yourself—is critical in doing great advocacy work. It's sadly rare these days.

———

As with any significant piece of legislation, we knew that we would need a substantive body of evidence to present at a hearing. Hearings are held to discuss an issue or explore the pros and cons of a particular piece of legislation. The chairman (a member of the majority party) lays out the subject of the hearing and then invites stakeholders and experts to give their views. There is always a panel reserved for the minority party, and frequently they use it to present the opposing viewpoints on the issue or bill under consideration. Normally a hearing will have three panels over a two-hour period. The administration is usually afforded at least one slot, if not an entire panel. The committee staff selects witnesses. Every member of the committee is allowed to make short opening comments, and all are allotted time to ask questions of the witnesses. Frequently, massive amounts of data are entered into the record through the committee process, creating a robust resource for future actions or research. When lawsuits are filed against bills or around the meaning or interpretation of a law, the hearing record is an important element that courts review.

In this instance we had little time to arrange an elaborate program of witnesses to present an in-depth case. So, as chair of the Senate Health Committee, Kennedy decided to take matters into his own hands. In December, while most senators were back home enjoying winter recess, Kennedy and Michael visited hospitals, clinics, and social workers in Kentucky, San Francisco, Los Angeles, and Chicago. As part of this tour, they talked to everyday people fighting AIDS. Kennedy returned utterly convinced that if we didn't act on AIDS soon, we would face the impending collapse of urban medical centers.

Our strategy emerged quickly. We would introduce CARE in the Senate, where Kennedy was an enthusiastic champion and chair of the Health Committee, and where we had the support of the ranking Republican, Orrin Hatch. This combination ensured a fairly smooth passage through the committee process and intrigued all who paid attention to the odd couple of Kennedy and Hatch working on AIDS. We didn't have the resources to fight for two bills simultaneously, so our strategy was to pass a really great bill in the Senate and then use that momentum to work with the House.

In February 1990, Kennedy, Hatch, and twenty-six other co-sponsors introduced S. 2240, the Comprehensive AIDS Resources Emergency (CARE) Act of 1990. Elizabeth Taylor joined Kennedy and Hatch for a widely covered introductory hearing and press conference to announce the bill and promote its swift passage. It was a bit surreal that morning as I walked to the Ritz-Carlton on Massachusetts Avenue to meet Elizabeth Taylor and brief her for the testimony she was about to deliver in the Senate. I'd drafted most of her remarks with Michael's help and with that of Taylor's assistant Sally. While Taylor was incredibly generous to give us her time and celebrity to launch this historic moment, she came with a bunch of must-haves, like first-class airline seats with no one beside, in front of, or behind her (that's four first-class seats!); similarly in hotels—a suite was needed, no other guests beside her or above her (that's a suite plus three other rooms to rent); she never liked to be awakened before eight a.m., and she required three hours minimum to eat and dress. The Senate had set the hearing time for ten a.m. and Taylor would of course be first. Do the math: we had a problem! In the end Sally had her in the car at nine fifteen a.m. and promptly delivered to the Senate at nine forty-five a.m. I told her I admired her beautiful pearl necklace and matching pearl and diamond earrings. She calmly said, "Did you know, my dear, that I never wear any jewelry that is fake? All of this is real and I own it!" I laughed and she laughed, and to this day I'll quote that to my sisters and nieces when on special occasions they need to put the good stuff on.

The next day, we sent out an action alert to the NORA coalition, requesting letters in support of CARE. It seems so antiquated now, but back then it was cutting-edge stuff: in a few hours we could inform organizations and individuals around the nation that an important action was getting ready to happen (mostly thanks to our knowledge of votes in committee or on the floor). Once our action alerts hit the fax machines, massive phone trees and phone banks were deployed to help fill up phone lines and message pads with our support or opposition. When NORA got big that meant one action alert would go to 120 organizations who would then fax the alert to their field and they would begin the phone or letter campaign. At our best we could put a few hundred calls or letters in a congressional office within forty-eight hours. It was considered revolutionary back then.

All during March and April, letters poured in from AIDS service organizations all around the country. Efforts like this in other issue areas would have cost millions of dollars and taken years to create, so in this sense, the structure of the coalition worked brilliantly.

In early April 1990, the battle over AIDS funding had reached its zenith in the Senate. We were poised for CARE's markup hearing before the Senate Committee on Labor, Health, and Welfare. Despite Kennedy and Hatch as co-sponsors, the long-term prospects didn't look good. Even though we hadn't yet realized it, we needed help. We needed a superstar. And we found him in Ryan White.

It was not until the morning of the bill's markup in the Senate committee that the pieces fell into place. The markup was to begin at ten a.m. in the committee hearing room in the Dirksen Senate Office Building. We gathered there early that morning to brief Senator Kennedy on what to expect. Because Senator Orrin Hatch was an original co-sponsor and also the committee's ranking Republican, he and his senior staff joined the briefing. It was Senator Hatch who suggested the bill be named in honor of Ryan White. At this point, Ryan was dying. A week earlier, Ryan had been admitted to the Riley Hospital for Children in Indianapolis with a severe respiratory infection. He had to be placed on a ventilator and sedated.

While we immediately agreed that this was a noble idea, I remember worrying that we might offend Jeanne by using the public's sympathy for her son to gain political traction. I suggested that Senator Kennedy call Jeanne to ask her permission. I had no idea how she would react. Here she was, this young single mother from small-town Indiana, whose family had been thrust into the national spotlight just five years earlier. Now she was at her son's deathbed about to be interrupted by a relative stranger (albeit one of the most powerful politicians in the country) six hundred miles away in Washington who wanted to use her dying son's name to help win a fierce political battle over AIDS policy.

Senator Kennedy and Senator Hatch each spoke with Jeanne briefly and explained the situation. "Well, I'm not sure what to say," I remember her saying. "I mean, I guess that would be great. Ryan would be honored—*we* would be honored. That would be terrific. Can you do that? Will this really help?" Secretly, I wondered if Jeanne truly understood the enormous act of generosity she was committing and the legacy that Ryan's name would bear. But Senator Kennedy hung up with a satisfied smile. "Let's get to work," he said as he stood up abruptly and headed toward the committee room. He strode in, called the committee to order, and without hesitation, they renamed the bill for Ryan and put the final touches on the most important AIDS legislation ever considered by the US Congress.

It wasn't until we were ready to bring the bill to the full Senate the following week that we ran into problems. Senators Jesse Helms, Gordon Humphrey, and Malcolm Wallop and a handful of other Republicans said they would immediately block it from going to the floor, and George Mitchell, then Senate majority leader, acquiesced, saying he "just didn't know" if he could find time in the Senate calendar to withstand a filibuster. A filibuster is a unique privilege in our democracy for the Senate. The Senate operates on a principle of unanimous consent. That means that no bill can proceed to the Senate floor unless all senators agree to the rules by which it will be debated and amended. This allows every single senator the right to have their voice heard on any bill. If any one senator objects to proceeding to a bill, it stays in the cloakroom until a negotiated agreement is reached. In the old days, there were rare times when one senator or a few or even the opposing party would object. In such a case the bill's sponsors can go to the floor to invoke cloture—the chamber petitions its members over seventy-two hours to see if sixty members (a supermajority) agree to proceed to the bill without the unanimous consent agreement that is typical. After seventy-two hours a roll call vote is taken, and if the bill sponsors get sixty votes to proceed, they may then proceed to debate.

In the 1990s, filibusters were rarely used, and they were considered an extreme tactic in legislative negotiation. Those seventy-two hours represented precious time, which would not be squandered for a losing cause. The clock was ticking: we had to pass the bill in the Senate, get it through the House, and then get it through a conference committee by September in order to get it signed before the federal budget was completed for the year. We might well get the entire Congress to agree on a huge new AIDS program—only to miss the budget negotiation and therefore lose out on funding.

The stakes were as high as I had ever experienced, for two reasons. First, the budget and appropriations process only happens once a year (it's supposed to be by October 1 each year). If you miss the deadline, you wait a year to get in line for funding the following year. In 1990, a year's delay meant thousands of lives lost and perhaps the bankruptcy of some of our more fragile AIDS organizations. The second looming threat were the budget hawks, mostly Republicans. They were circling closer and closer to a deal that would cap spending each year, thereby halting the capacity to fund new programs and services. Their idea was that you had to cut other programs to create or fund new ones. They never applied these rules to the Department of Defense or to tax breaks for the wealthy, but they were looming over the spending for domestic programs for health, education, welfare, agriculture, and so on. I was keeping a very close eye on this threatening storm, and I knew the clouds were building. I feared that one year later we'd be living under caps that would not allow us to draw large new spending amounts. We'd be stuck, or we'd be at war with all our colleagues doing domestic social program work—a dilemma I dreaded.

I went to Senator Bob Dole's office—he was then Republican minority leader—and met with his chief of staff, Sheila Burke, to see what could be done. Sheila had been a nurse and understood the severity and human toll of the AIDS crisis and was, as a result, very generous and cooperative. She was also in charge of the very delicate task of protecting the rights of Republicans as the minority party. Though she was harshly criticized for it—even years later—Sheila helped us figure out how to isolate Helms and his colleagues so we could get the majority of Republicans to go along with Ryan White. Sheila assured me that we had to prove that we could mobilize a super majority (sixty senators) to break any attempt at a filibuster by Helms. As it stood, we had barely forty co-sponsors, and the list was largely Democratic. I buried my head in my hands and sighed. I had a queasy feeling that good might not prevail this time.

Then, something both tragic and miraculous happened. That Sunday, April 8, Ryan White died. News of his death reached the major news outlets before I even had a chance to call Jeanne. Knowing she would be flooded with calls of sympathy and with the painful business of funeral arrangements, I decided to wait a week before reaching out. Finally, on April 16, I called her and listened to her describe her last few days at Ryan's bedside. She finished, and I remained quiet for a moment. Then, I began, "Jeanne, I know this is a difficult time...and I'm not sure how to even ask this...but we need you here in Washington. We don't have the support we need yet for the CARE bill, for Ryan's bill, and I need you to come and talk to some senators here."

With little hesitation, she said, "Okay, I'll come—but I can't leave now; I have to do laundry." We agreed she'd leave the next day. I hung up and called the airline to book her ticket for the next flight from Indianapolis. Realizing suddenly that we didn't have a working credit card anywhere in our possession, I ran around frantically asking everyone I could think of for their credit card number. They must have thought I had finally lost my mind. Thankfully, a donor to AIDS Action came through.

I picked Jeanne up late the next day. With no organizational funds for hotels, we hosted her in our guest room that night, and the next day we took a cab straight to the Capitol. I briefed her on the way over. She asked only a few questions and was calm and quiet. I sensed something had shifted in her. She seemed stoic and anxious. We arrived at the Senate entrance to the Capitol Building and began to climb the sprawling marble steps that lead to the main Senate chamber. It was then that she had that first incredible conversation with Senator Biden.

The rest of the day flowed in a surreal fashion: as senators came out of the chamber, we picked them off one by one. By eight o'clock that evening, we had gone from forty-two senators co-sponsoring the bill to sixty-one—one more than the magic number we needed.

We gained more than just Ryan's bravery, or his sudden celebrity, when he lent his name and spirit to the CARE Act. It helped us circumvent the misinformation, hysteria, and rampant homophobia associated by many with the disease, since most Americans viewed Ryan as an innocent who contracted this deadly illness despite doing nothing wrong. These are not and were not my thoughts, but those prejudices mattered in the politics of the moment. Even so, Ryan and his family embraced the gay community and rejected this dichotomy of innocent versus guilty. Ryan made it clear that AIDS was no divine retribution for immoral acts of homosexuals, and he made it impossible for legislators to ignore the disease. Looking back, I wonder if there were forces at work beyond our understanding. I can't help but think that Ryan White's death—and the grief of so many other losses that we spotlighted on the Hill—were sacrifices that took CARE from a pipe dream to a reality and changed history.

Despite Jeanne's heroic efforts in building a filibuster-proof majority, we still had a ways to go. I asked Jeanne if she could stay a few more days. She agreed. Then I called Tim Sweeney in New York. He said he would send out an alert immediately to GMHC clients' family members to see how many would be willing to come to Washington on short notice. We bought seventy-five seats on an Amtrak train car and started loading people up in Boston, then continued on to New York, Philly, Baltimore, and then finally DC. At each stop the car filled with friends and family members of people who were living with, or had died from, AIDS. Jeanne White marched the group of mostly middle-aged and elderly women straight to the Senate visitor's gallery, where they stayed until Senator Mitchell came to the floor around seven p.m. and announced that he would call up the CARE Act. We had survived the first several rounds of political wrangling. When the final vote came on May 16, it passed hands down—ninety-five to four in favor, with one not voting. But we were far from cracking open the champagne. Once CARE suddenly looked even more viable, people started coming out of the woodwork with requests.

These were very explosive times. The high-stakes dynamic created political theater and opportunity. One major source of drama was the group ACT UP, an extreme left-wing activist group. The stunts they orchestrated that spring as CARE was weaving its way through Congress were legendary. There were two back-to-back outrageous pranks, in particular, that are worth recounting.

On May 21, 1990, ACT UP stormed the campus of the National Institutes of Health, throwing blood around the lobby and breaking down the door of the director's office. It was unclear to all but the ACT UP members if this blood was human and if it was infected with HIV. In fact, it was pig's blood and posed no threat, but it horrified NIH scientists and bureaucrats. I got a good talking-to by members of Congress, who reminded me that they were inclined to be supportive but *not* if the community continued these kinds of antics. The following September a group of ACT UP members created a giant condom (out of latex balloon), rented a cherry picker truck, and stretched it over Senator Jesse Helms's home in suburban Virginia. This stunt got me more than a few tongue-lashings from senators in both parties.

Sometimes, ACT UP would even target us. The job of the activist is to demand and push the margins; the job of the lobbyist is to get a majority while holding on to key principles but knowing you have to compromise to get the votes to win. This understandably resulted in some tension between our two groups. Once, when Pat Christen was pregnant and giving a presentation, an activist ran onto the stage and dumped a box of used cat litter on her head (an obvious attempt to scare her, since toxoplasmosis, which cats can carry, can be harmful to fetuses). On another occasion, at a meeting at AIDS Action's offices, the local ACT UP group burst through the doors and handcuffed all of us to the conference table—trying to symbolize the fact that we were complicit in handcuffing people with AIDS to outdated regulations that kept lifesaving treatments off the market.

Every time ACT UP pulled something new, I tried to use the opportunity to remind members of Congress that unless I could work with them to produce some modicum of progress on AIDS policy, actions like this were likely to persist. While the left wing was mostly about street theater and rage, about disrupting ambivalence by shocking people into attention, the right wing expressed its opposition in an overtly political fashion aimed mostly at fund-raising and winning elections. Over time, as I spoke with more members and their constituents, I began to realize how turned off most people were by both extremes. The crazier the crazies became, the more members wished to be associated with a moderate middle ground.

I began to develop what I call the airplane theory, which is a simple rule for managing issue-based campaigns. It goes like this: To fly an airplane, you need a left wing and a right wing. If either wing is missing, the plane won't fly. The smart strategist recognizes that they are the pilot. The pilot's job is to manage the rage by allowing—even facilitating, if necessary—an irrational left wing in order to pressure the right wing to make concessions. Meanwhile, the pilot can use the presence of right-wing ideologues to encourage politicians to support a more moderate position. Novice strategists frequently spend too much time and create too much drama trying to control the extremes. My advice is simple; you can't control it, so use it!

In the case of the Ryan White Act, allowing the left to shout and the right to make demands made both sides feel like they were being heard. This ultimately allowed the bill to represent a true moral consensus in a way that few other bills have since then. Orrin Hatch wanted to help people who were dying, even though he is a fiscally and socially conservative Republican; Kennedy saw the great injustice of the AIDS epidemic and used his considerable skill and reputation to address it. On the House side, Henry Waxman was a master legislator and a human being with a great heart. He also was politically secure and confident in taking on issues that for many were controversial but for him were the right things to do. But the story of AIDS in the US and particularly in the politics of the US Congress cannot be written without the passion, contribution, and leadership of two congresswomen from California: Barbara Boxer and Nancy Pelosi.

After CARE passed the Senate, we waged a similar battle on the House side. The process for moving legislation in the House is much simpler than the Senate. House bills go through the Rules Committee, and they decide how a bill will be called to the floor, what amendments will be in order, and what the time and debate allocations will be. When a bill leaves the Rules Committee, all the legislative maneuvering is planned. In this context especially, the powerful Democratic chairman of the House Subcommittee on Health Henry Waxman was a master. He got the bill out of his subcommittee past a Helms-like Republican named Bill Dannemeyer. He got the powerful Democratic chairman of the full committee, John Dingell, to push the bill through committee, which is one of the most intense moments when negotiating a bill to its final version.

Politics always matters in a committee process, but it is at this level when the substance takes its most serious and aggressive reviews. Committee markups can take days to complete. Every member of the committee from both sides of the aisle reviews the bill (sometimes line by line) and is offered a chance to amend the bill. Usually the staffs of the majority and minority try to streamline this, and a lot of backroom negotiation can occur as staff and members prepare for markup, but the process is designed to be precise and intense. Not only do you need to be prepared to defend or defeat something on every line of the bill draft, you always become acutely aware of the politics. Committee markups are clear indicators of where the opposition is going and what they are likely to choose to fight on when the bill gets to the floor. A great strategist prepares aggressively for markups and pays careful attention to all the details and subtle politics if they are smart. Whatever doesn't get resolved in committee is likely to be attempted at Rules (in the House) and then on the floor. The privilege of democratic processes like this (when they work) is that you're never really defeated; there is always a chance to win in the next phase. In this case, Dingell's staff director Alan Roth deserves some credit—a gay man, but not out totally, Alan took some risks to help us find safe passage. In the House of Representatives, if an amendment isn't cleared by Rules, it can't be offered on the floor. This is very helpful in not getting surprises or poison pills on the floor. A poison pill is an amendment to a bill that is either so clearly outrageous or unconstitutional that an opponent adding it to the bill will either spell death by vote or litigation before implementation. Both are recipes for disaster on progressive social change legislation. Once we cleared the Rules Committee, we were on our way. The House ultimately voted 408–14 in favor of HR 4785.

The next step was to work out the differences between the House and Senate bills and to send a final version to President Bush for his signature. The conference committee staff began its deliberations on Father's Day weekend. I had promised my dad a sailing trip to St. Michaels, Maryland, on the Chesapeake Bay, using my newly earned captain's certificate. I told everyone that I would be unreachable for the weekend, but that was not to be. As the Sheridan clan—all seven of us—set sail on a beautiful June Saturday, my mom went to the galley to prepare lunch. Making meals while underway in a close-hauled sailboat is not easy—it requires you to balance at an angle and to keep your dishware and food from sliding to the floor at every tack. I went below to check on her, and when I returned to the cockpit, my dad had the wheel (he had been in the Coast Guard and loved the sea but wasn't formally trained as a captain). As we tacked around a place called Bloody Point, a fast-moving Coast Guard vessel was bearing down toward us. I noted it but didn't for a moment think they were actually coming for us. Then they slowed and came directly to the starboard side of our boat. I let out the sails to slow us down, and the Coast Guard came in closer. I was growing more nervous by the second. I was a new captain, my dad without a license was at the wheel, and I knew getting boarded by the Coast Guard isn't really good news. An officer yelled, "Is there a Tom Sheridan on your vessel?" I answered, "Yes, that's me." "We have an urgent message for you to call Senator Kennedy via your ship-to-shore radio: do you understand?" "Yes," I replied, and they sped away. You can imagine the look on my family's face. I went belowdecks and did as I was instructed. By ship-to-shore radio I called Michael's direct line in the Senate. Michael was brief. He said there was a problem in the conference committee and he needed help. Ship-to-shore calls are expensive, so I asked if I could call him from St. Michaels in two hours. He agreed. When we arrived in St. Michaels, I spent the next three hours on a pay phone at the dock while my family relaxed on the shore. When I got back to the boat, my mother simply said, "You really should have taken my advice and gone into hospitality."

After several more days of back and forth, the House and Senate approved the final version of the Ryan White CARE Act of 1990 on August 4. The only thing left was to make sure President Bush signed it—which was still far from a given. Some members of the Bush administration didn't like the way the CARE Act was crafted. It was very prescriptive, and it forced federal action in very fast time frames. There had been times in writing the bill when I had deep cooperation from people embedded in the agencies, but I'd also had some of the more political types threaten me with veto warnings. Up until that moment I'd ignored them; now I could not. In a very matter-of-fact way, I told Bush's chief counsel Boyden Gray that, should the president choose to veto or threaten to veto the bill, ACT UP would join forces with Jeanne White and all of the mothers who'd come to the Senate, and they'd meet at the front gates of the White House to express their outrage. He listened politely, and I never heard any more objections.

Bush finally signed the bill on August 18 while on Air Force One somewhere over Missouri on his way to Texas. The administration had refused to do a public signing in the White House or to let Jeanne come to the private signing. I will never know whether President Bush was determined to spite us or if his staff recommended that he not sign the bill publicly. The pettiness of it all left us with a bitter taste, but we didn't need White House fanfare to understand the magnitude of what we had accomplished.

The day the Ryan White CARE Act was signed into law I left my office at AIDS Action and drove with Vince down to our summer home in Lewes, Delaware. I go to Lewes often to gather myself, rest a little, and think. I remember arriving that late summer afternoon, getting a glass of wine, sitting down on the front porch with our golden retriever, Crosby—and crying. I honestly don't know why I cried. I'm Irish; we don't cry unless it's watching coffee commercials at Christmastime. I think it was mostly happiness, a sense of pride and relief, and an expression of the grief I felt for so many but didn't have time to reveal. All of it came over me in that one quiet moment. I knew that what we did was remarkable, but the awareness that is was historic would come later. At the final moments of this great victory, I was only looking at the future and hoping to do more.

Second View: Michael Iskowitz

It's the job of a Senate committee chairman's staffer to help shape and find sixty-plus votes for effective solutions to major social challenges. Such was my task as counsel to Senator Ted Kennedy in the early days of AIDS, when fear had frozen compassionate action against the epidemic on Capitol Hill.

In the face of a rapidly escalating body count, gay men and allies in highly impacted cities across America had begun creating volunteer-driven community-based care networks that brought help and hope to individuals living with HIV. After years of keeping these networks going and growing largely through private donations, communities had developed a model service delivery system that both responded to

---

the extraordinary human need and reduced pressure on public hospitals on the brink of collapse, and they brought it to Washington for replication and expansion.

Senator Kennedy and I witnessed these homegrown efforts during field hearings from coast to coast and so began a partnership that led to the enactment of the Ryan White CARE Act (RWCA). Along the way, I learned some important lessons.

Compromise isn't always a dirty word. Compromise gets a bad rap. Senator Kennedy always said we should never compromise our values or principles, and we should never fail to explore a compromise on a process or program. That advice holds true in plenty of circumstances outside of politics.

In its best form, compromise represents a win-win situation that allows people with different perspectives to all feel good about a policy result, which wouldn't happen without broad-based buy-in. Such was the case with the RWCA. While initially the focus of the act was disaster relief for hard-hit cities, the AIDS epidemic was more quietly unfolding in small cities and rural communities in America's heartland and the deep South. Senator Kennedy and I saw this firsthand when we spent a day in a one-room schoolhouse outside of Waycross, Georgia. Once a month this building was transformed into a makeshift clinic for hundreds of people living with AIDS in surrounding communities. Many came lying down in cars covered with blankets so that no one would see them and their telltale sores. Responding to challenges in both the visible urban hot spots and in "invisible" rural communities not only made policy sense; it connected many more senators to the enactment of the RWCA.

Relationships matter. One serious casualty of the current polarization on Capitol Hill is real relationships across party lines. RWCA would not have happened without relationships that allowed senators and staffers to disagree with each other on policy but still maintain respect for one anothers' humanity. My friendships with Nancy Taylor, counsel to Senator Hatch, and with Sheila Burke, chief of staff for Minority Leader Dole, were indispensable. Their genuine belief in the need for action against AIDS was central to our collective victory. While it was Sheila's job to make sure that all Republican senators' views were considered, including those who desperately wanted to stop the RWCA, she is also a big-hearted nurse who was determined to find a way for the important work against AIDS to prevail. Nancy Taylor was key to finding the balance between urban and rural interests that enabled Senator Hatch to be a lead sponsor of the bill, which she did while skillfully

HELPING THE GOOD DO BETTER

enlisting her Republican colleagues—and while very pregnant with twins. They both frequently told me that we should hug in private so that we didn't "blow our cover" as adversaries. To this day, I would walk through fire for them.

The power of making people feel. From the beginning, the RWCA bill was blessed with many assets. These assets included an extremely broad and active coalition of mayors, governors, doctors, nurses, hospital administrators, public health professionals, faith and business leaders, AIDS activists and service providers, a congressionally appointed AIDS commission, and a smart and tireless coalition leader who wouldn't take no for an answer. Supporters also included Elizabeth Taylor, a living legend. Many senators were huge fans of hers, and the fantasy of seeing her in person led them to flock to the bill's introduction, even though the price of admission was signing onto a multibillion-dollar AIDS care bill. She sent letters to senators on scented purple stationery, reminding them of what she needed them to do. We always had to laugh when we saw a senator stumbling around all misty-eyed smelling one of those personal notes.

Yet, despite a 14–0 vote in committee, months went by with no floor action, and each day more Americans died of AIDS. Senator Kennedy told me to find ways to push past people's fear and get them to feel, to tap into their empathy and transform it into an openness to act. Then came Ryan, a beautiful teenager with wisdom well beyond his years—a face of AIDS that America couldn't turn its back on. In his short life he had endured all of the fear and ignorance that came with AIDS, and his response was simply: love bigger.

When Ryan was in the hospital, Senator Kennedy and I called to check in. Elton John, who had been doing a vigil by Ryan's bedside, answered the phone and gave us the news that Ryan had slipped into a coma. When we hung up and returned to a committee meeting of senators, Senator Kennedy told the story, and when we talked about what was to become the RWCA, Senator Kennedy said, "This one's for you, Ryan!"

Ryan's call to action made all the difference, as did the willingness of his mother, Jeanne, to come to Washington soon after his death. She came to remind senators that it was not only about facts and figures but faces and families, opened hearts and minds. Ryan made people feel, and by doing so, he turned the tide.

TAKEAWAYS

My involvement in the AIDS lobby proves that activists don't need vast political experience or deep pockets to influence public policy. We didn't begin with a grand plan or a huge bank account; we started with a few inexperienced AIDS service providers unclear about how to best take action, huddled in a conference room for two days. But we focused immediately and intently on two questions: What could the federal government do to make the local response to the AIDS crisis more efficient and effective? And how could we press public officials into action? Looking back over the three years we spent lobbying for CARE, plus the last two decades spent fighting for the bill's funding, several overarching lessons emerge.

First, understand where your issue stands in the public eye, and adapt accordingly.

Is the issue on the public's radar? Is it important to constituents back home in members' states or districts? Is it ripe for political action, or does it first need a catalyzing moment in order to appear on people's radar? If we hadn't addressed the effect that AIDS was having on mainstream society—the tendency to categorize AIDS victims as either "innocent" or "guilty" and to dish out punishment or mercy accordingly—we would have failed. That's why we constantly reframed the argument for AIDS funding in the context of public health. We ran a research, civil rights, and care agenda, but left prevention off the table. If we had tried to tackle everything at once, we would have set ourselves back on the entire AIDS agenda for another four or five years. But because we understood that the AIDS care issue had the qualities of a crisis, we could frame our ideas as a rare opportunity to act boldly.

Second, don't be afraid of tackling a severe issue with relatively few resources.

The severity of your issue can make it more relevant to the general public. And your lack of resources can make you more resourceful, innovative, inclusive, and dynamic. Ironically, when the odds seem impossible, it may actually be the best time to act. We were severely resource constrained. This forced us to aggressively leverage every ounce of political, financial, and human capital—wherever we could find it. Had we been flush with grants we might not have pursued coalition organizations like the American Medical Associations or the American Nurses Association, which were very influential voices on the Hill because of their credibility on medical issues. Ironically, having little money made us more effective.

Third, your greatest adversaries are often your greatest teachers.

Neither Helms nor ACT UP were close colleagues of ours; both were adversarial. But I appreciate today more than ever how much a conservative opposition teaches you to sharpen your game and to do your homework (i.e., opposition research). A radical left, on the other hand, keeps you honest and grounded, and forces you to ask yourself if you are compromising too much, moving too slowly, or not thinking boldly enough. People showing up at demonstrations carrying their lovers' dead bodies reminded us quite vividly and on a daily basis that people died when we screwed up or sold out. Such raw, honest emotion helps keep you truer to the community for which you are fighting. For social advocates and coalition builders today, this means that you must go to your most direct stakeholders and encourage them to keep you honest, thoughtful, and innovative, even if they annoy the hell out of you and disrupt your life—that's their job.

KEY QUOTES AND LESSONS

- If it's good enough for Mother Teresa, it's good enough for you.
- Take risks, especially when you are young. You will learn a lot and maybe accomplish more than you imagined.
- You need a left wing and a right wing to fly a plane; you need the same to run a movement.
- Find allies wherever you can—and look in unusual, out-of-the-way places. You might be surprised.
- Ryan said on *The Phil Donahue Show*: "In my case it was fear, and just because, you know, I supposedly had something in my body that nobody else had, or very few people had. And I think it's just because you're different. I mean, I'm surprised we really have dogs nowadays be-

cause they're different. It's amazing how, you know, you can accept a dog into your house, but you can't accept someone because of their race, you know, their color or their religion or what they have in them."

THE THREE P 'S FOR THE FIGHT AGAINST AIDS

Policy: We wrote the Ryan White CARE Act from a strong place: we focused on the needs of people living with the disease and their local service providers. We never forgot that, and it grounded our work in substance and context.

Politics: We threaded the needle carefully, using the passion and urgency and anger of ACT UP and others to help push us, while also using the common ground of CARE to bring both sides of the aisle together. We needed and used every AIDS volunteer, staff member, family member, doctor, nurse, and social worker who offered to help. People power was our political power.

Press: Ryan put a face on the epidemic and created a legacy for the bill. Rock Hudson helped gain attention. Elizabeth Taylor got the lights, cameras, and action, and demanded that reporters pay attention to our solution. All of this brought the public in and validated our work and our ideas.

CHAPTER 2

Debt, Trade, and Extreme Poverty

"A rock star, a Kennedy, and a social worker walk into a bar..."

ONE WARM DAY in May 2001, Ted Kennedy called me out of the blue. My first reaction, after being thrilled, was that I was a little bewildered. By this point I had come to know Senator Kennedy, but not in a "hey, how you doing," casual-phone-call way. I was just an awestruck kid when I first met him in the late eighties, and our relationship had grown more solid during the Ryan White and ADA days. In 1992, when he married Victoria Reggie, she and I became friends by working together on gun control issues. My partner, Vince, and I began to cross paths with Victoria and Senator Kennedy socially; we hosted dinners they attended, and they returned the invitation by welcoming us at special events over the years. I even got to sail with them on Kennedy's beloved yacht *Maya* off the coast of Cape Cod.

One especially treasured memory is of a dinner at our

home in DC a few years later in early 2008 where the senator insisted—rather unequivocally—that I not compromise by replacing a wood mast with a faux-painted aluminum mast on my almost-completed sailboat, a dream long in the making. He told me, "Look, on a beautiful evening after a lovely day sailing you'll be on shore and looking back across the marina and there you'll see her, the sun shining on her mast, and it will glow gold—a beautiful color that only a wood mast can achieve. And in that moment you will say to yourself, 'I have the prettiest girl at the dance.'" I had to admit he had a point. I told him I looked forward to having the Senator and Vicki come to Lewes for a weekend to sail with us when the boat was finished.

That day never came. Two months later, Senator Kennedy had just been diagnosed with brain cancer when I christened my boat *Ceili* and sailed her to Lewes. At sundown I was sitting on my porch admiring my new boat and as the light hit it just so, the mast glowed in gold, just as he promised. I grabbed a camera, took the photo, and sent it to the senator, just released from the hospital and recuperating at home in Hyannis Port, with a thank-you note including his quote at the bottom. To this day, when the moment is right and the sun is setting, I can hear his voice and am grateful for his advice, for I do have the prettiest girl at the dance.

Vicki has sailed with us, an able member of the crew. She is also captain of a beautiful Herreshoff wood sailboat named *LaBoheme* given to her by her husband and named for the opera they went to the night they were engaged.

In any event, on that day in May when the senator called,

the call was less than thirty seconds long. I couldn't really hear what he wanted me to do through his clipped speech and thick Boston accent, but it sounded like his nephew Bobby wanted to talk to me about working with Bon Jovi on AIDS. It didn't really matter what he was asking; when Ted Kennedy called, you said yes.

A few days later the phone rang again, and I told the rock star on the other end of the line that one big challenge on these issues would be explaining to members of Congress why a rock star from New Jersey cared about AIDS and poverty in Africa. That's when he interrupted. I was nervous I'd offended him when there was a long pause. "New Jersey? I think you may have me mixed up... This is Bono. I'm from Ireland—have you heard of U2?" Well, that made more sense. In 1999 Bono had called Eunice Shriver, whom he had met at Special Olympics, to enlist her help in getting Senator Kennedy to assist in the US government leading on a millennium initiative to drop the debt of third world countries. Eunice did not connect Bono to the senator but instead recommended that he talk to Bobby Shriver, her son, about this project. Bobby and Bono had known each other through working together on *A Very Special Christmas* album the year prior but I think he was unaware that Bobby was also a former executive at the World Bank. According to his mother, Bobby was perfect for the job.

Despite the awkward start we soon became a team—Bono, Bobby, Jamie Drummond, Lucy Matthew, Scott Hatch, and me. The slipup did me no long-term harm. Over the next fifteen years, I recalled that conversation with Bono more than once, along with other funny moments shared over late-night meals and long plane rides. We shared tense moments when huge sums of money and thousands of lives hung in the balance. To this day I stand in awe of one of the best examples of credible engagement by a rock star or celebrity I've ever witnessed, one I believe serves as a model for any celebrity or cause that wants more from the relationship than fund-raising and one-day society column stories.

———————

After my time working on the ADA and the Ryan White Act, I decided to make it a priority to pull back and take some time to evaluate what I wanted to do next. I started the Sheridan Group right after leaving AIDS Action, and it was time to reassess. I wanted whatever came next to be meaningful, to make a difference to other people, and to be personally rewarding. But I wasn't naïve: I knew if I wanted to make it in Washington, I had to be shrewd and calculating and make friends with the right people. I also decided I wasn't going to be a one-trick pony or a single-issue guy.

I'd be committing a lie of omission if I didn't say that some of my calculations about my next move were a little less than saintly. I needed to make a living, and more than that, I needed money to mount a campaign for Congress in New York in 1994, a lifelong goal. That was my reason for opening a consulting practice: I had no intention of building a business or a firm. It was a tactic in a strategy, a means to a larger end—to pursue public service in elected office. But as fate would have it, I found that my first clients were not only passionate about great issues but also great leaders and soon fast friends. My practice wasn't developing a business model as much as it was developing into a series of relationships that tapped into a personal sense of commitment, loyalty, and satisfaction. The fulfillment of working with others in a creative and energetic practice—free of dysfunctional boards in particular—was freeing and exhilarating.

I'd also like to say that I came to the idea of working to help the world's poorest people rise up out of poverty on my own—but in reality I was pushed. Hard. The guy doing the pushing was someone I couldn't ignore, and the idea was presented in a brilliant way that made me think we actually had a shot at success. Vicki Kennedy had mentioned me to her nephew, Bobby Shriver, as someone who might be able to help with AIDS and debt forgiveness for the poorest countries in the world, in particular in Africa. The truth was I didn't know anything about AIDS in Africa, and nothing at all about debt forgiveness. I actually tried to tell that to Bobby, but he didn't listen.

My relationship with Ted and Vicki Kennedy was already a long-standing and meaningful one. I got to know the senator when I worked at the Child Welfare League of America—he was a champion of a number of bills I worked on, including the Abandoned Infants Assistance Act and the Fair Housing Amendments Act of 1985 (which protected families with children from discrimination in rental housing). I got along with his staff very well, and his staff director Tom Rollins was very kind to me and my causes. I grew even closer to his health team through our work together on AIDS, particularly Michael Iskowitz and Terry Beirn. Vicki and I became friends after she married Ted, and we worked together on commonsense gun policy.

Aside from the fact that I'd do most anything Ted Kennedy thought was a good idea, it turned out his nephew Bobby's mission was one that I immediately recognized as worthy: debt forgiveness for the poorest countries in the world. When developing countries borrow money from the World Bank or the IMF (and often they have no choice due to the pressures of free trade agreements and other factors too complicated to lay out here), they are required to pay back the original amount borrowed plus interest. As a vicious cycle took root in the 1980s and 1990s, most of the money African nations were receiving from foreign aid was going to paying back previous loans instead of supporting the starving, impoverished people who desperately needed help. Thanks to compounding interest, by 2000 and 2001, for every dollar the countries in Africa borrowed, they owed eight dollars: no country, no matter how economically robust, could pay back that sort of debt. Forgiving national debts would enable countries to make use of their own natural resources; build infrastructure like roads, railways, and schools; create better access to food and health care; and set the path for a new generation free from the cycle of poverty. The idea of debt forgiveness had picked up steam as the new millennium approached and Pope John Paul II had declared the year 2000 as a Year of Jubilee: a time of releasing people from bondage and debt.

The concept of a jubilee connected to economic concerns and serving as a time for release from bondage has been around for thousands of years—and the year 2000 provided the development community an opportunity to hop on board, taking the lead of the religious community and heralding this as the perfect moment to forgive third world debt.

Bono was first approached by development advocate (and now close friend) Jamie Drummond, who later became the executive director of DATA and then director of global strategy at ONE. A part of the cause from the very start who remains dedicated to this day, Jamie has provided the second view on this issue, which you will find at the end of this chapter. Jamie knew of Bono's wildly successful involvement with the Live Aid concerts some fifteen years earlier, organized to help with famine relief in Africa. If you're old enough, you might remember the anthem "We Are the World" or watching Mick Jagger create a wardrobe malfunction for Tina Turner by practically ripping off her dress. The epic Live Aid efforts raised $200 million. But Jamie made the point to Bono that one single African country, Ethiopia, paid $500 million every single year to service the debt it owed to the World Bank and IMF. It was time to do something more.

And so they did. Jubilee 2000 was a coalition formed of American faith-based organizations that were attempting to solve this problem. Their efforts were proving fruitless until Bono and Bobby joined the effort and enlisted the help of Congressman John Kasich, the chairman of the House Budget Committee. The result was a remarkable achievement, the US Congress committing $769 million to multilateral debt relief and promises from Tony Blair and the UK to get to 100 percent debt forgiveness for the world's most heavily indebted poor countries and to convince other members of the G8 to do the same. The new millennium had begun, the issue of debt forgiveness was in the headlines, but the work was far from over.

––––––––––

Bono and Bobby's relationship was now forged and their commitment was solid. As to how Bobby Shriver came to this work, he virtually had no choice: he had it in his blood. The son of Sargent Shriver Jr., who started the Peace Corps and created President Lyndon Johnson's War on Poverty programs (e.g., Head Start, the Job Corps), and Eunice Kennedy Shriver, who founded the Special Olympics, Bobby was raised to believe that helping people, on the biggest scale possible, was not only doable but morally necessary.

Bono and Bobby both saw extreme poverty and AIDS as two of the most perplexing challenges facing the developing world but in particular Africa. After the success of the millennium debt-forgiveness campaign, they took the next step of founding the group DATA—"a double acronym meant to position the group as a nexus between the nonprofit development world (debt, AIDS, trade, Africa) and the results-oriented political world (democracy, accountability, transparency in Africa)." Of course, the name was meant to also indicate a no-nonsense, just-the-facts approach to getting things done.

And Bobby knew that to get anything done in Washington they'd need to hire professional lobbyists and strategists. Bono was an extraordinary guy—and he was aware of the power he could wield—but he didn't know how Washington worked. He did, however, have some friends in high places on the Hill, including John Kasich, a Republican congressman from Ohio. Bobby and Bono started asking for recommendations; they needed lobbyists to work with both the Republicans and the Democrats. Kasich recommended Scott Hatch, a former Republican leadership staffer, and Bobby's uncle, Senator Ted Kennedy, recommended me to deal with the Democrats. When I came on to this cause, I knew my devout Catholic grandmother would be proud. No one less than the pope himself was already behind this one.

Scott Hatch and I came from dramatically different political circles. Scott was a huge U2 fan—and still is. I, as you might have guessed, didn't have any great working knowledge of Bono's day job, but I loved his passion, brilliance, boldness, and devotion. In any event, both Scott and I were deeply practical and fiercely political, so we got along very well. Luckily, there were a few other hardworking and supremely smart people in the trenches with us. Jamie Drummond was now working with Bono full-time on his advocacy and public interest agenda, and we also had the help of Lucy Matthew, Bono's chief of staff. Tom Hart, lead lobbyist for the Episcopal Church and a leader in the Jubilee campaign, joined the DATA staff about a year later.

We got started in earnest in 2001. The big push to Jubilee 2000 was over, and we now had a George W. Bush administration to contend with. Bono had made good inroads during

Clinton's administration, with the president even agreeing to erase $6 billion in third world debt thanks in no small part to the Irishman's haranguing. But the sad truth of how Washington really works was a lesson Bono hadn't yet learned. As a *Time* magazine piece later noted, "Bono was very pleased with himself until he learned that he hadn't actually accomplished anything that would make its way into law. Congress hadn't signed off." The article then quoted him saying, "When I first arrived in Washington I asked, 'Who's Elvis here? Who do I have to speak to to change the world?' Then I find out that even though the president says yes and even though he speaks with a twang, he's not Elvis. Congress is Elvis in America."

When Bush took office in 2001, most people in the development world feared that third world debt and AIDS in Africa were going to be shoved to the bottom of the agenda. Bush himself had basically said as much. But our team was undeterred. We would do as much as we could as quickly as we could—while we had some momentum from the previous administration. We figured out early that our value to the new Bush administration was to connect our ideas to his campaign theme of being a "compassionate conservative." In that simple connection we found ample political capital to move big ideas and big money into our agenda. Bono had already created credibility with Christian conservatives thanks to Jubilee 2000, and his uber-celebrity status helped us broker the ideas behind DATA as a continuation of Bush's Christian-tinged idealism in the White House and on Capitol Hill.

Bono had already made twenty-four trips to Washington, DC, before he began working on what would become DATA, all below the radar screen. But even so, our commitment at DATA was to maintain a very low profile as we began work. Bono openly told members of Congress he knew little to nothing of the American political process but was willing to learn in exchange for a fair hearing on his idea to alleviate suffering from poverty and AIDS. The humility factor was second in value only to Bono and Bobby's determination to stick with this issue and to do hard lifting. They were in it for the long haul. This was not red carpeting, or a photo op, or a PR stunt—it was a sincere long-term commitment to serious work and their dedication and commitment was inspiring.

Bobby had a simple motto for DATA that we all adopted: "We get the check!" That meant our job and our focus wasn't to create programs or offer services; our job was to apply political pressure to fund programs and find new ways to accelerate progress on AIDS and extreme poverty. Our agenda was right there in our name: debt (making sure we stayed on track with the Jubilee 2000 debt-relief promises), AIDS (getting lifesaving drugs to those who needed them but couldn't afford them), trade (looking for policy ideas to build economies), and Africa (our geographic focus). Our discipline to clear ideas with serious merit allowed us to move quietly at first within the highest levels in DC to build relationships and support for the DATA agenda.

From the support we built in the White House, we knew we had to next tackle Congress. Nancy Pelosi, the Democratic leader and member from San Francisco, had always been a champion for AIDS—we found a home in her offices and a willing coach and leader. The Pelosi family are huge U2 fans, but even she needed to be convinced of Bono's sincerity at first. It didn't take long. She hosted Bono's first formal Democratic meeting on Capitol Hill for DATA—it was a lunch in her offices with eight democratic leaders. The agenda was to introduce Bono and the DATA agenda to Democratic leaders and to seek their counsel in moving forward. As minority whip of the Democratic caucus, Pelosi had a beautiful dining room just off the rotunda in the Capitol Building. With plush mahogany furniture and large chandeliers, it was the classic power Washington lunch space. Leader Pelosi is the consummate hostess, true to her Italian roots: every guest is treated with the utmost in gracious, generous hospitality. Bono got the full treatment: china, silver, flowers, and tablecloths. Even as a rock star Bono remains pretty humble and frequently refers to his roots in the "lanes of Dublin" (Irish for slums). He was suitably impressed.

Nancy Pelosi had done her best, and we worked hard on our end to choose the right number of members from all the right parts of the Democratic caucus. We had agreed beforehand on the flow of the conversation at lunch—a flow brilliantly facilitated by Pelosi. It went off without a hitch: Bono was in true rock star advocate form, impressing everyone with his smarts on the issues and his sincerity. The members were honest, direct, clear, insightful, and committed. Representative Dick Gephardt, the Democratic leader of the House, told Bono a heartfelt story of his first trip to Africa to see the devastation of AIDS firsthand. His impressions were still fresh—raw, in fact. "Come here anytime and lobby as hard as you can," he said to Bono. "We need that. But if you can get any member of Congress to go to Africa and see what poverty and AIDS really look like you'll never have to lobby them again—they will be in your corner for life." Bono for his part spoke directly of his personal time and experience in Africa and why poverty had become such a passionate issue for him. He riffed about Ireland being a country (one he loves) but about America being an idea (something quite bigger than just geography). It was at this lunch that I heard him for the first time talk about AIDS and security, telling members that if people in Africa saw "red, white, and blue drugs arriving to save their lives—they'd be fans forever." It was a wild success.

Building on this first lunch meeting, Bobby had the idea to set up some bipartisan dinner parties. We came up with some very odd groupings that included various senators, former World Bank president Jim Wolfensohn, former Treasury Secretary Larry Summers, and, often, Queen Noor of Jordan. The idea was to break down barriers and convince those in attendance that if they could find commonality on something, it would be this. It also helped to make them look like team players and set off a few press flashbulbs on their behalf, and we got support for our cause. Bono understood his role in the equation perfectly, and he was more than willing to do it. He knew that his superstardom could be converted into something of real and lasting value, something that mattered.

It worked. We had an undeniably righteous issue, helping improve the lives of some of the poorest people on earth. We had one of the biggest rock stars of all time not only supporting the cause but also crusading—pleading with legislators to do their part to relieve the debt in order to free up those resources that would help save and improve millions of lives. We had dedicated staffers working long hours. And following the mantra "We get the check!" gave us amazing clarity to go do the job. Other organizational interests or constraints didn't hamper us.

To give a little bit of context, charities that are labeled as 501(c)(3) tax-exempt organizations are prohibited from using money for political purposes. This includes limits on what they can do and spend on advocacy campaigns for issues and not just in the electoral space—it applies to activities across all aspects of government (legislative and executive branches). Being a 501(c)(4) means you are allowed to do more aggressive issue advocacy, including unlimited lobbying, but donations to a 503(c)(4) are not tax deductible, which makes raising money more difficult. Most mature issue-based organizations have both operating so they can have as many options in the advocacy toolbox as possible.

Since DATA began as a 501(c)(3) in 2002, it required more political muscle. We opened it as a 501(c)(4) in 2003 with personal donations from Bill and Melinda Gates matched by AOL. Our clear intent was to build bolder political and policy work. The flexibility to engage in unlimited lobbying and more aggressive issue advocacy was transformative in this space. These unique capacities allowed us to go big and bold. It created some envy from the major health NGOs operating in Africa, but it was a very clear gift that we used effectively.

We also very purposely built not only bipartisan champions but also constituents for those members that mattered to them back home. That was not easy—Republicans clearly don't share a constituency with Democrats. For the Republicans the base was evangelical Christians, and on the Democratic side it was young people. Our near orthodox adherence to always have both sides on the same page and to getting equal amounts of time and thanks from both was sometimes maddening, but it was worth it and paid large dividends in the end. We were so committed to establishing Republican champions that Bono and Bobby flew commercial to Sonny Callahan's district in Alabama to meet with his best friend, the guy who owned the Ford dealership—that is humble lobbying at its best.

And in the middle of it all, Bono was playing his other role: as the front man of one of the biggest bands on earth. He got on a bus and did the Heart of America tour across the American Midwest to demonstrate the need to get Americans engaged. This turned out to be my year as a roadie, as the U2 management had agreed to give us backstage access at concerts as a way to increase our support with key members of Congress and senior staff. The one requirement was that we manage the guests ourselves and be there to guide them through the venue. When we made the agreement that seemed like a reasonable request, but little did I know how tough life on the road with a rock band could be. Every time someone wanted to go to a show, I had to fly to that city to help them and then fly back to DC to do my day job. Although this turned out to be exhausting, it did give me the opportunity to meet a lot of interesting people, as Bono often hosted late-night hospitality drinks with friends.

One night in particular, I had gotten to the venue early

to brief Bono on the political guests we would be bringing backstage before the show. Outside his dressing room, there was a handsome stranger sitting there. Wanting to be polite, I introduced myself and told him I could let Bono know he had someone waiting. I walked into Bono's dressing room and said, "There is a man out there named Tom Brady who says he's your friend. Do you want to see him?" I was a little embarrassed when it turned out this particular Tom Brady was a famous football player—I had no idea who he was! Bono laughed so loud I kept urging him to stop because I was sure Brady would hear us.

There are lots of other, less embarrassing stories from my time on the road, including when we ordered delivery pizza from the tarmac outside a small private plane. The look on the delivery driver's face when he realized he was delivering a pizza to Bono on a private jet was priceless. I think Bono's favorite story is about being in a diner in Iowa. A truck driver approached, more as if looking for trouble than an autograph. "You're Bono, right? I hear you're working on AIDS in Africa," the trucker said. "If you need a driver to get those drugs to people who need them, I'd volunteer to help." Bono was awestruck, but replied simply by saying there was surely a challenge in getting drugs to people in remote areas of Africa but that the trucker could best help by telling political leaders to help find the money to buy AIDS drugs and get them delivered. "Can you help us out with that?" Bono asked. "You want me to tell my senator to support funding to fight AIDS?" asked the trucker. "Done—that's a lot easier than driving a truck in Africa." Everyone laughed. That tour, and the conversations it sparked, proved to Bono that Americans could and would rally if we did the hard work of asking them for their support.

———

Our hard work paid off: the United States gave three times as much aid to Africa during the Bush presidency than it had before, reaching a sum of about $4.3 billion. In the lead-up to the G8 Summit in Scotland in July 2005, President Bush pledged that US aid to Africa would double again by 2010, to $8.6 billion per year. About $2 billion would be directed to the landmark President's Emergency Plan for AIDS Relief (PEPFAR). What's more, G8 also agreed "that all of the debts owed by eligible heavily indebted poor countries to IDA, the International Monetary Fund and the African Development Fund should be cancelled."

It was almost difficult to imagine bigger success. But of course, making a promise is much easier than delivering on it. We had to keep at it, holding leaders accountable for their remarks and pledges and relentlessly pushing: by courting their staffers to earn their trust and by finding ways to keep the issues on their agenda. Part of our efforts included publishing reports on the state of the epidemic and effects of the interventions, something we still do today. As time went on and success swelled, we knew we needed a way to create a more robust organization. Our mission was still to get the check, but as our success for improving budgets and appropriations line items grew and policy initiatives like the

Millennium Challenge Corporation and PEPFAR passed, there was a growing restlessness in the traditional NGO community—"coopetition" of sorts raised its head (we'll get more into coopetition in chapters to come).

One story about the launch of the Millennium Challenge Corporation (MCC): Bono had agreed to stand with President Bush at the White House as the president announced what would become the MCC initiative just prior to a G7 meeting in Mexico. The outline would be rolled out, but they were not going to commit to any particular money goals at this press event, nor were they willing to do it privately with us. The night before we'd been up late at a suite at the Four Seasons in Georgetown arguing if Bono should go or not. For hours the phone went back and forth between Bobby and Condoleezza Rice, the national security advisor at the time. She kept pressing Bono to come; Bono kept pressing back that he wasn't comfortable standing up for a plan that didn't have money committed to it. She pledged that she had tried as hard as she could but couldn't give us a commitment for dollars. She asked Bono to "trust her and trust her boss." They hung up. Bono asked, "What can I do? If I say no, I say I don't trust them. If I say yes, I could get used." The core team debated and I was squarely in the "don't do it without money" camp. My counterpart and friend Scott (the Republican) pressed him to "take the deal." In the end Bono went to the announcement.

Nearly a year later, in 2003, after PEPFAR was passed and the president was sending his budget to Congress, we got wind that they weren't going to adequately fund the bill—their request for funding would be substantially below what we'd called for and passed in Congress. Bono came to DC, and we scheduled a meeting at the White House in the Oval Office with the president, chief of staff Josh Bolten, and other aides. Bono pressed for a commitment to minimal funding needed to get PEPFAR off the ground. Bush hedged, dodged, and explained that there just wasn't enough money to get all the way to our goal. Bono was agitated, respectful but displeased. He explained his trust in Bush when he took the photo months earlier and why now he'd have to fight back in Congress if the numbers were too low. I was not in the room (Democrats weren't allowed, but Scott was). I waited outside the north gate for them to come out. They did—hurrying down the driveway past the press waiting at the stakeout area outside the West Wing entrance. I knew when I saw them that something hadn't gone well.

They jumped in the car. Bono summarized what happened. We were due to cross Lafayette Park immediately after to meet, talk, and report the meeting's progress with all our NGO partners at St. John's parish hall. They were waiting, and we were told the press was there as well. We drove around the White House compound three or four times, debating what to do. Scott was worried. The tone of the meeting was tense, and he was pulled aside by Bolten and warned that if Bono went out against Bush, we'd pay a price. I stuck to my one point—they asked you to trust them, and you did. You took the picture. Now they have betrayed that trust. Your job isn't to be their friend; it's to hold them accountable and to win—we must fight back and say so publicly now. I lost that first debate at the Four Seasons, but I won the SUV fight. Bono agreed, and we hurriedly brain-stormed some remarks on a yellow pad in the back of the car. He brilliantly changed the sentence "I just had a rather robust fight with President Bush" to "I just had a row with the President." *Row* is the Irish word for fight, but it can be said in a more charming and humorous tone, which is exactly how Bono used it.

Reference to that row set off a series of very angry calls from the White House to all of Bono's supporters in DC, including members of our team. The heat went up—high! I got calls from most of the senior Democrats, like Nancy Pelosi and Tom Daschle, congratulating Bono for his courage and his commitment to fight. That night was tense for all of us. The next day we went to Capitol Hill to really take the row to where it would matter—Congress. We won the budget battle. Years later, after Bush had left the White House, Josh Bolten, who was then on ONE's board of directors, invited Bono for dinner at his home in Great Falls, Virginia. When I spoke with Bono the next day, he told me that Bolten told the gathering, "Bono, it was singularly the best thing you ever did to hold our feet to the fire that day. Had you not done it, PEPFAR never would have had the money it needed and none of us would be talking about it as the game changer it is. I didn't like it then, but I'm damn proud of it now."

As DATA's work grew and the politics got complicated, we realized we needed to reorganize. We had created ONE as a coalition in 2004, and so in 2008 we combined DATA and ONE into one organization and kept the name ONE. I helped with organizational development issues a bit more, but my overall role did not change; I was still the lead Democratic strategist.

By 2012, (RED)—the brainchild of Bobby and Bono—would also be merged under the ONE umbrella. (RED) was a hugely innovative idea that also crossed traditional boundaries, in this case between business and humanitarian aid groups, paving the way for the growing ethical consumerism or conscious capitalism movement. The idea was simple but brilliant: companies like Nike, Apple, Coca-Cola, Gap, Hallmark, and many others create a product and give it a (RED) logo, and then donate up to 50 percent of the profit when the product sells. It was also politically necessary, as the Bush administration was pressuring us to bring in private-sector money as part of the overall commitment on global AIDS. All of the donated profits go to the Global Fund, which was created in 2002 to raise and invest funds to support large-scale prevention, treatment, and care programs for AIDS, tuberculosis, and malaria. A huge portion of all funding worldwide to treat these diseases comes from the Global Fund, due in no small part to the money from (RED). American Express even tested a "red card" in a limited market, mostly in the UK; it didn't work out, but the card still sits on my desk as a reminder of the power of new ideas. DATA, and even Bono, could not get everyone engaged. (RED) products, and their companies with large marketing budgets, were capable of putting us in every mall in America, and this helped.

Today ONE is a very large and highly visible brand in international advocacy. It has offices in London, Berlin,

Nairobi, Tokyo, and Ottawa, and a staff of more than two hundred. Bono remains the leader and a dedicated advocate. Bobby is on the board. Jamie is a senior advisor but in reality remains Bono's go-to guy on all things public interest. At the end of 2015 we helped pass the Electrify Africa Act—one of the only pieces of bipartisan legislation to emerge in the 113th Congress. Nearly 70 percent of sub-Saharan Africa's population does not have reliable electricity. That means no reliable lights, lifesaving hospital equipment, or food refrigeration. Imagine the implications for sanitation, health care, education…the list goes on. That bill will help provide electricity access to 50 million people for the first time.

To be with Bono in the same room for some of the most interesting and colorful moments in the history of ONE has been a privilege. Bono's meeting with Jesse Helms—the ultra-conservative homophobe who had been my archrival on domestic AIDS issues—was a watershed moment and perhaps one of the most difficult and interesting in my career. Helms's co-sponsorship of PEPFAR cleared the way for nearly all the Christian conservatives in the Senate to join the effort, but being in the same room as him was awkward to say the least.

As an aside, watching John Kerry give away the base ideas for what became PEPFAR to President Bush was perhaps the most generous act of political statesmanship I've ever witnessed. After we had created a relationship with the Bush White House and saw the opportunity to make AIDS in Africa the embodiment of his "compassionate conservative" message, we needed to find the legislative vehicle to roll it out.

Nancy Stetson, John Kerry's longtime Senate Foreign Relations Committee staffer, drafted an early version of PEPFAR, and John Kerry introduced it, but by 2002 Republicans had the majority and we knew it would have to become a Republican bill to get the White House on board and the Senate in a position to move it. Bono personally led the effort. With very graceful facilitation, Tom Daschle, the Senate minority leader, worked with John Kerry to give the base bill to Bill Frist. Passing the torch to Frist, the new Republican leader (and a doctor), allowed the Bush Administration to embrace PEPFAR (though they amended the bill in some significant ways—adding abstinence provisions, for example). To this day I don't think Nancy Stetson and John Kerry get enough credit for their early work and their selfless political decisions.

Back at ground level, working with ONE opened many doors for me careerwise. Bobby Shriver is one of my biggest fans, and I return the esteem. He promotes our work in many sectors, and my relationship with him opened up a wonderful door to collaborate with his brother Mark Shriver at Save the Children. Getting involved with ONE helped shape the Sheridan Group—credible celebrity management brought us some attention, but the utilization of those assets actually created the real change. We frequently counsel our clients to be careful not to see celebrity engagement as a moment but rather an asset to the movement.

The true definitions of bipartisanship and nonpartisanship

were crystalized through my work with ONE. We got stuck with ONE on the idea of being bipartisan—thereby allowing the Republicans more often than not to essentially veto our ideas or actions just by simply not showing up. From that I learned to not so easily give up the capacity to run our own campaign by allowing any party to simply not participate. Instead, I now strive to be nonpartisan, which means you choose what you are going to ask for, and then you get support from whoever is willing, regardless of their political party. This concept would become critical as my career progressed and I tackled more decisive issues.

The ONE story matters because it is perhaps the best example of credible celebrity engagement I've ever witnessed. I believe it is the model for any rock star, celebrity, or cause that wants more from the relationship than fund-raising and one-day society column stories. There's nothing wrong with either of those, but they are not advocacy work and they don't bring about transformative social change. If you want to do advocacy, you must have a sincere commitment to the cause for the long term and the humility to learn and fail in the rough-and-tumble world of politics. The truth is, Bono is unique as a celebrity advocate. Though we have engaged with other stars for other issues, the experience has not been replicable, no matter how eloquent or attractive these stars may be.

The story of Bono and ONE is also a story about clear vision and goals. As Bono said in an interview with Larry King in December 2002, "Two and a half million Africans are going to die next year for the stupidest of reasons: because it's difficult to get the AIDS drugs to them. Well, it's not difficult to get fizzy drinks to the furthest...reaches of Africa. We can get cold, fizzy drinks. Surely we can get the drugs." He knew how to make a powerful argument—and how to sell, sell, sell.

Despite the enormous success of ONE over the years, there are challenges ahead and more work to be done. Many things conspired to bring ONE to its successes, but the times have changed, and success going forward cannot be replicated using the same strategies and tactics. We need to be able to define our political relevance to each new US president, and that remains the single biggest challenge for ONE moving forward. To continue to make a difference ONE will have to remind itself of its early disruptive roots and replicate them anew in a world still burdened with extreme poverty and AIDS. ONE's work won't be over until we solve these two things and truly "make poverty history." We have come a long way, but there is still a lot of work ahead.

Second View: Jamie Drummond

Tom Sheridan is what many would call a mensch and what the Irish call a sound feller. There's no higher praise. Here's why.

When I was an even younger campaigner than I am now, I turned up in Washington, DC, with big ideas, a few well-connected friends, and a total high off a huge campaigning win—we had just helped secure billions in debt relief for the world's poorest

---

countries to celebrate the year 2000. This win had been secured within DC by great leadership from characters like Bobby Shriver, Bono, and Tom Hart as well as congressional champions on both sides of the aisle and some folks in the White House.

But, being campaigners, this win wasn't enough. Throughout the 1980s and '90s, while these countries' cold war debts had been accumulating interest, the HIV/AIDS crisis was raging rampant, especially across the content of Africa. All the progress that could come from debt cancellation stood to be destroyed by the AIDS crisis, and worse was to come if the pandemic wasn't stopped. We explored how we might take some of our momentum on debt and turn it into action to end the AIDS crisis. Getting serious cash was going to take real political capital in Congress, as well as presidential leadership. That's when Bobby's network (and especially that of his mom, Eunice) helped point us in the Sheridan direction. We had heard of Tom's expertise in marshaling the domestic AIDS lobby for the Ryan White CARE Act, and knew we needed that kind of deft drive to build bipartisan support. And we needed it fast. Back then 5,000 people died from HIV and 6,500 caught it every day, mainly in Africa. ARV drugs existed—those modern miracles—but they were way too expensive for average people, let alone African citizens.

And so the campaign began. Tom's hand was at the tiller both in guiding key Democrats toward the issue and in partnering with Scott Hatch to help get key Republicans involved, by being sensitive to the needs of moderate and some less moderate Republicans whose support was vital to win key votes. The Kerry-Frist Bill blossomed into new life as the President's Emergency Plan for AIDS Relief, via strong support from the legendary senator Jesse Helms as well as Hillary Clinton, Pat Leahy, and the uncompromising Rick Santorum. Thanks to the efforts of lesser-known heroes and heroines on both sides, 15 million people are on ARVs, and 1 million fewer people are dying every year from AIDS because of the global aid response led by the USA and powered by bipartisanship that now seems elusive, led by people like Tom.

Along with Mort Halperin, Tom became a personal mentor of mine and a great friend, too, despite him being fond of repeating the saying "If you want a friend in Washington, DC, get a dog." It's true that I found DC to be a less-than-welcoming place at times, between the stress of campaigning and the isolating fact of losing friends for associating with President Bush. There are certainly some souls in DC who need to get out of the Beltway a bit more. In Tom I had more than a friend in DC—I had a mensch and a sound feller, indeed.

TAKEAWAYS

Assuming you're not going to be hanging out with any megastars soon, what sorts of lessons can Bono teach the rest of us working in the world of advocacy or social justice? Here are some simple lessons you can use whether your goal is to raise funds for the local food bank or gin up enough support to run for office. I like to call this "How to Choose Your Superstar—or Become One Yourself."

First, having a leader is great, but you also need a vision.

Some believe that the simple act of hiring a lobbyist or an in-house policy director is the first and last step in a process—some outsider with special expertise who can come in and fix things. This is incorrect. Organizations must actually think about mission change and decide on goals and a direction before looking for an expert or headliner to help institute large-scale changes or launching a new campaign.

Second, it helps to have a rock star, but what you need most is a road crew.

Bobby Shriver and Bono helmed DATA and now the global group ONE, but they couldn't get anything done without all of the legislators, advocates, policy wonks, and development experts who work with and for them. Similarly, most organizations and nonprofits that are successful in policy and advocacy engage the entirety of the organization's assets in this work. These hardworking folks are your roadies, the people who show up every day and get stuff done. They study the cases, iron out the details, earn and schedule the meetings, and make real change possible. Without their expert work, the voice of those headliner rock stars would never be amplified or broadcast; they might know the songs, but they don't know how to work the sound equipment to make their voice heard by the millions.

Third, this work is an epic tour, not a one-off gig.

Policy and advocacy are a relationship-based effort. Much of my work with Bono was done in the back of a car prepping him for meetings with people who would become crucial partners. Your capacity to earn the trust and respect of your elected officials will not come overnight. As nonprofit advocates, we don't have the privilege of money and campaign donations that our corporate counterparts do—but, in my opinion, we don't need them. Your strength is in your work and the impact you are having on the communities you serve. This unique political power must be developed and nurtured over time. Simple actions like regularly showing up at town hall meetings, asking for district-based meetings with your members of Congress, and offering them a tour of your program and a chance to meet your clients (who are also their constituents) are simple ways to begin meaningful and productive relationships with policy makers, and they are all within the boundaries of the law.

KEY QUOTES AND LESSONS

- Forge your own path. Bono used this quote in a commencement speech at the University of Pennsylvania in 2004: "If you want to serve the age, betray it." (That's one of my favorite lines of poetry of all time, from the Brendan Kennelly poem "The Book of Judas.") Every generation has had its moral blind spots. But what one generation struggles to discern clearly will no doubt be viewed by their children in brilliant daylight.

- Be undeniable and tenacious. In this case our mission was pure, but the politics were complicated. There were plenty of times people said no to Bono, but he kept going. When trying to do important work, tenacity matters. Sometimes what happens after someone says no actually matters more in proving your commitment and creating a path to success.

- Humility is sometimes more powerful than hubris. Bono's early work was all about saying what he didn't know, being willing to learn, accepting political challenges, and agreeing to conquer them.

- Opening doors isn't the hard part; knowing what to say and when to say it once you're in the room is the talent. Bono didn't need me or Scott to get him any meetings, but he trusted us to choose those meetings for their strategic importance in pursuit of clear goals.

THE THREE P'S FOR ONE

Policy: Our most successful policy win was and remains PEPFAR. It was already a policy idea in formation (with John Kerry and his staff), but it became PEP-FAR after some additional policy work and political compromises were forged. It really stands as a testament that great policy work is often the meeting of extraordinary substance and unparalleled political courage.

Politics: The key here was finding the opportunity for Bush to equate being a "compassionate conservative" with supporting a major policy on global AIDS. When presidents require something political and advocates can match that with bold substance and transformative policy, great things can happen. But advocates have a political role to play, too, and if Bono hadn't kept Bush's feet to the fire on funding, PEPFAR would have been a worthless paper promise and Bush wouldn't have had his most popular legacy item. This moment also saw incredible bipartisan partnership and selfless acts of courage. It's been nearly fifteen years, and I haven't really seen anything like it since.

Press: Bono didn't need any help getting press or attention, but when and how he used this power of celebrity was careful and disciplined. His work and messages were always carefully chosen to advance real policy work and address critical political moments. I think his Heart of America bus tour may be my favorite "press" moment. He truly went to the heartland of America and asked them for support. This is how you use the press to bring the public along.

CHAPTER 3

The Americans with Disabilities Act

"The stone soup of politics: coalitions"

IT WAS a late May evening in 1990, and I was sitting in a small room tucked up inside the dome of the US Capitol Building, Ted Kennedy's hideaway. The most senior members of the House and Senate are given small rooms inside the upper floors of the Capitol Building. Senator Kennedy rarely used his for meetings or public events; instead it functioned as his private domain, a place to get away from distractions and read or write. It was a beautiful room with a large fireplace, deep sofas, comfortable chairs, and a desk he was comfortable working at. I was working on both Ryan White and the Americans with Disabilities Act at the time, and we were nearing the final push for both bills. Senator Kennedy had invited the leaders of the ADA to meet with him and Senator Tom Harkin, the primary sponsor of the ADA, to discuss the final floor strategy and to make some sensitive decisions on our way forward.

We were warmly welcomed into this inner sanctum by Senator Kennedy, and I stepped in with reverence. I was especially awestruck by the hundreds of photos that hung on the walls and graced every flat service. Childhood photos and notes from his father, mother, and brothers were framed and lovingly placed. There were sailing trophies and political memorabilia, but that night my first thought was, *This is a very real person who loves his family and his comforts.* While all of those surroundings evoked history and maybe even celebrity, the awesome nature of just being human is what still remains with me today.

But our task that night was not social or human or casual. We had a serious problem. An amendment had been passed the afternoon before in the House that was threatening the entire Americans with Disabilities Act, and this amendment was unfortunately uniquely targeted at me. Congressman Jim Chapman (D-TX) had proposed an amendment to exempt people with HIV/AIDS from the ADA, and I was not sure we had enough votes to get the amendment removed.

It was late, everyone's nerves were frayed, and a decision had to be made. The final vote in the Senate on the Americans with Disabilities Act was due to take place the following morning. After two hours that felt like a lifetime, Kennedy brought the conversation to an end and then looked at me and said: "It's your call. You've done the vote count. Is there anything you think you can do to get those final votes?"

The decision before me was huge—should we amend the bill by striking Chapman, or should we kill the bill that everyone had worked so hard on? I knew we didn't have the votes to win at that moment, as we were two to five votes short of a majority. Further complicating things was that an amendment to strike Chapman meant that the bill would be changed and would have to go back to the House, and they very well could include another similar amendment. It was like a tennis match: the ball was in our court. It was the biggest decision of my career to date, and I knew it. Leaving the building that night was scary—everything depended on how the next morning would go, and I had to make the crucial decision. All I could do then was hope my ADA colleagues and our congressional champions would agree.

A lot had led up to that long night with Senators Kennedy and Harkin. In some ways it all started with my very first job, as a social worker in charge of opening group homes for people with developmental disabilities in New York. Then Reagan got elected. Suddenly I got letters from the federal government to every one of my group homes saying that overnight, the residents had become "un-disabled." They didn't fit the definition any longer, because the definition had changed on them. Because they were living in a community and working in community jobs—which was the whole goal in getting them out of institutions—they no longer qualified as disabled. This ignored the fact that residents' rent was paid with their Social Security disability income, their food through food stamps, and trips to the movies and other kinds of leisure activity were paid for by their incomes from community jobs. The Reagan budget cuts tightened the rules; they said that disabled people could not be capable of living in a community like ours. If they were able to do so, they would no longer be eligible for the programs we relied on. The social policy house of cards that the homes were built on looked like it was about to collapse.

In order to save the group homes, I organized a huge backlash against the budget cuts. Our first line of defense was actually the clients themselves; we had ensured that they were all registered to vote. Second in line were their parents and family members, and third in line were our staff and the members of our board. We had been through fights with zoning boards when we began setting up the group homes, and so we were well aware of our friends and allies, including other populations and service providers who were also facing the same crisis. Our entity was called the Coalition on Block Grants and Human Needs, and we came out swinging. We had a Republican member of Congress at that time in New York, and I got people to go to every town hall meeting he had. People were writing letters and going down to DC, making a big loud fuss about the budget cuts. Looking back, I would say we were about 75 percent successful: we were able to push back on many of the major eligibility changes, but we still suffered from across-the-board budget cuts. This was one of my early experiences with advocacy: the press around it and my role in the advocacy caught the attention of the National Association of Social Workers, and they gave me a fellowship and a full-tuition scholarship to get my master's degree, which is how I ended up in DC. So in a way, my advocacy career has always had disability rights at the heart of it.

———————

Three years later, when I was working at the Child Welfare League of America as the deputy director, I was able to make my own portfolio of policy issues. It was very important to me to be able to focus on issues relating to children with disabilities. In addition to my time working at the group homes, I had a personal connection: I have both a cousin and a niece with Down syndrome. My aunt used to tell the story about the day her son was born. The pediatrician said, "Don't name him; we'll just take him away. You'll never have to know what happens, and don't bother yourself—he won't live very long, he'll never walk, he'll never talk. He'll be taken care of in an institution until he dies, which will probably be soon. Just pretend this never happened." That's not the path my aunt chose. But that sort of "disappearance" happened to hundreds of thousands if not millions of others.

By the time my niece was born in the spring of 2001, the situation had changed for the better, and I was honored and delighted to be asked to be godfather to my sister's third child. When the doctors told my sister her baby would have Down syndrome, it was a much more positive experience, and my sister knew her baby girl would still be able to lead a full life.

Colleen was born on St. Patrick's Day in 2001, the morning after a party to celebrate the tenth anniversary of the Sheridan Group. We were all gathered at my home for brunch when the news came that Colleen had arrived early. We were prepared, but the excitement and the love that morning when she finally arrived, safe and healthy, was a very special moment. My mom, Irish Catholic and not prone to lots of displays of emotion, broke into uncontrollable tears of joy, and most of us followed suit. Passion for issues usually comes from personal experience, as mine did for the disability community, and it can and does deepen when the effects are personal. I have often told seminars of people interested in advocacy that the fiercest advocate is the parent of an ill or disabled child—they are simply a force of nature, and I know why.

———

People tend to have the impression that the disability rights movement came out of nowhere, but that could not be further from the truth. The basis of the ADA can be found in the civil rights movement of the 1960s as well as the women's rights movement. Members of the disability community had been working on disability rights legislation for years—the first real victory came in 1968, when the Architectural Barriers Act was passed. The ABA required that all buildings constructed using federal funds must be accessible to all physically handicapped people. Standards of accessibility had been around since the 1950s, but this was the first time accessibility was going to be enforced.

In 1973, the Rehabilitation Act became the first law to extend civil rights to people with disabilities. This act prohibits discrimination on the basis of disability in all federal agencies and programs. After the Rehabilitation Act, things sped up. In 1975, the Education for All Handicapped Children Act decreed that all schools accepting federal funds must provide equal access to education for all children with physical and mental disabilities. Next the United Nations declared 1981 to be the International Year of Disabled Persons and recommended that all member nations establish their own organizations for people with disabilities.

By 1988 I was a member of the Consortium for Citizens with Disabilities, and we were working on the reauthorization of the housing rights act; one of our main goals was getting in provisions to prevent landlords from discriminating against people with disabilities and families with children. At the time I was also beginning my transition to AIDS Action, which dovetailed with my work on the ADA in some expected and some surprising ways. By the time the ADA was being discussed, I was sitting at the table with the other leaders of the disability rights movement as we began putting our strategy together. From the start, it was important to me to get civil rights for all people with disabilities, not just certain groups of disabled people. I had firsthand experience with the power of advocacy for disability rights, but I also knew that not all groups of disabled people had that power behind them.

If you ever want to see what advocacy does and doesn't do, look what happened under the same deinstitutionalization policy to two different populations. There was a huge difference between the success stories of people with developmental disabilities and the stories of people who were mentally ill. The parents of the developmentally disabled were fighting for the rights of their children; they were going to DC, writing letters, petitioning Congress, raising money. People who were mentally ill just didn't have those kinds of resources behind them. The deinstitutionalization movement for the mentally ill was a travesty, plain and simple. We still haven't solved the problem of homeless mentally ill people, forty years later. For people with developmental disabilities, there certainly were challenges, but they did not suffer the same sort of callous disregard and horrible consequences as did people with mental illness. In the 1970s, by the time you could get someone institutionalized for mental health issues, their families were totally burned out; they didn't have any more resources or patience or ability to support someone in need. I wanted to put advocacy to work for the more marginalized groups of disabled people.

When people started discussing the ADA, I and others felt strongly that the ADA should be for all people with disabilities—no exemptions. I'm not going to say it all went smoothly. The disability rights movement had its own politics. Traditional disability rights groups had been working together for years, and suddenly here we were, the newcomers: people with AIDS and people with mental illness. The disability rights community had been very focused on a specific subset of people, and now we wanted to open it up to groups that were a bit more politically problematic. This unity of the disability community would be tested time and time again as we went through the slow process of getting the ADA passed.

Before we could even think about passing legislation to protect the disabled, we needed to form an organization to begin crafting it. We ended up forming a remarkable in-kind coalition where a variety of people from different organizations all worked together. Ralph Neas of the Leadership Conference on Civil Rights co-chaired the coalition with Pat Wright, and his close relationship with political and civil rights leaders would be crucial in the difficult days that followed. We needed the support and enthusiastic political power of the traditional civil rights leaders—Coretta Scott King got on many planes, made many phone calls, and wrote more than a few letters of support for the ADA. Ralph's close relationship with Kennedy and many other political leaders was constantly used to consult, coordinate, and collude. I was the co-chair of the lobby task force, my friend Elizabeth Savage from the Epilepsy Foundation was in charge of the grassroots task force, and Chai Feldblum from the American Civil Liberties Union was in charge of the legal task force. When it came down to it, though, Pat Wright really ran the show.

Each task force had its own focus; my group was responsible for everything that happened on Capitol Hill, including visiting offices, getting co-sponsors, asking for hearings, and counting votes. Everyone who participated in the coalition brought something to the table. We didn't have any independent money, so we each had to get money from our own organizations to fund our efforts. Many of us treated our ADA work as a full-time job; our home organizations paid our salaries, but our time was spent on ADA business. Everyone had their own connections to the government and their own resources from their organizations, and we were able to pool it to make change happen. On occasion we needed to pass the hat for special projects like ads, plane tickets, and so on. On those occasions most of us went to one or two major donors and pleaded for the needed amounts.

Keeping an in-kind coalition focused and functional can often be a difficult task. It is hard to keep all of the members accountable and make sure there is enough funding to keep working toward the goal. Other coalitions can rely on funding and support from one big group, or money from dues paid by the members, but our coalition could only use what the members offered. Luckily for us, we had our "general," Pat Wright, to keep everyone working together. Pat had been a part of the disability rights movement for years, and I knew her from our work together with the Consortium for Citizens with Disabilities. Pat was from the Disability Rights and Education Defense Fund, based out of Berkeley, and working on the ADA basically became her full-time job. We called her General Pat because she was more like Patton than pixie: gruff, tough, harsh, quick, determined, and focused. Her leadership style wasn't always appreciated by everyone, but to her credit, she was always fair.

Pat and I always got along very well: as a New Yorker from a big assertive Irish family, I'm not easily intimidated. Pat was the kind of person who worked hard to earn respect, which is something I really value. That is not to say we didn't cross swords—we did. There were times during the ADA when the results from a lobby day came back less than impressive—not enough new co-sponsors added, a coalition member or two that didn't show up for meetings as expected, amendments threatened, opposition unveiled or exposed. In those moments, reporting back to our HQ at the ACLU offices next to the Senate office buildings could be trying, loud, and confrontational, and sometimes ended with a few slammed doors. On occasion it could get personal—inside our small group of leaders friendships formed and frayed, romantic liaisons flared and fizzled, careers were threatened, and accusations of conflicts of interest had to be dealt with. We had moments of drama, but in the end we all showed up every day ready to do the work needed to advance the bill. We never formally named our group. Informally, it was just the ADA coalition; we never even had letterhead. We never got bogged down in formalities, and this was one of our strengths: the structures were all ad hoc or in-kind. The product is ample proof that the process, flawed as it was, worked.

———

Once we formed the coalition, the next step was to plan the launch of the bill. The CCD had laid the groundwork for what would become the ADA, and I had been a part of that, but it was now time for me to step into a bigger leadership role. It was an interesting time politically: we were right at the end of one Congress, and we were approaching a presidential election year in 1988. We wanted to make disability rights a major talking point of the next presidential election, so that the new administration would be ready to accept the bill. Our plan was to introduce the bill at the end of the current Congress, with the knowledge that we would not be able to get it passed in time, just to get the ideas out there.

Let me pause for a minute to give some background on the ins and outs of the process of introducing a bill. When change makers are plotting strategy, it's very important to pay attention to the ebb and flow of how policy gets done and, more important, how politics affect that environment. For example, Congresses are convened for only two years (on the even years). What happens inside those two years is unique. A bill introduced in one Congress that does not pass goes back to square one in the next Congress, and you are looking at a complete redo. Each time a Congress reconvenes, the players are different. Some retire; some lose reelection. The majority and minority parties can swap, taking with them powerful leadership positions and the gavels of committees that are vital to strategic planning. If you are proposing a bill, you need to gauge how much runway you have—win or lose—for twenty-four months.

Every two years every member of the House runs for reelection, meaning 100 percent of them run at the same time. The Senate is different; they have staggered terms where a third of the Senate runs for reelection on the two-year cycles, completing six-year terms instead of the two-year term of the House members. Complicating all of this is a presidential election every four years. The big sea-change elections tend to be during the midterms, those between presidential elections.

Change makers must be not only good historians, knowing when these changes tend to occur, but also great clairvoyants—skilled at predicting the future and betting on outcomes. I have seen this pay off handsomely for those who do it well and plan ahead for opportunity they predict or hope will come as the political pendulum swings. I have also seen the opposite: strategies not planned, opportunities lost, whole initiatives stalled because of mistakes or miscalculations on the ebb and flow of Congresses and administrations.

For most issue-based movements there is almost always a three-to-five-year minimum strategy framework for success. This can be a bit off-putting at first; it feels like a long time, but it is not. To introduce a bill takes time. To get both a House and Senate version adds complexity. To get co-sponsors requires months of effort. To get through sub-committees and full committees is painstaking work. And then, floor action is difficult—the tasks of getting time, managing amendments, dealing with partisan divides, patching up unforeseen potholes. Once both chambers actually get a bill done, you then go to conference—more pain, more compromise, more hijinks. Then you head back to the floor of the House and Senate before the bill can go to the president. If you weren't paying attention, you could face a veto. If you pass muster, congratulations, you have a bill passed.

But wait. Not so fast. In most cases the bill requires money in order to get a program operating, so you now need to start a budget and appropriations strategy. The bill authorized the spending, but you don't yet have any money. Now you need to get the actual check through an entirely different process with entirely different players. If it took two years to pass the bill (which is lightning fast), now you're in a new Congress trying to get budget and appropriations committees to provide the money. At the Sheridan Group we tell our clients that to truly play for appropriations, you need a dedicated, disciplined process that spans twenty-four months. Yes, the process is complicated and very competitive, but I can assure you that when you win, you have indeed made real and significant change.

Before we could get the wheels turning on any of that for the ADA, we needed to identify our supporters in Congress. This was one of the easiest parts of the process. All of our key leaders had personal connections to people with disabilities. Senator Harkin, a Democrat from Iowa, had a brother who was deaf and a family history of people with disabilities. Senator Kennedy's son, Teddy Jr., was disabled after losing a leg to cancer. (And his sister, Eunice, one of the founders of the Special Olympics, was passionate about disability rights as well.) Senator Lowell Weicker (R-CT) was our champion on the other side of the aisle—a Republican who had a son with Down syndrome. These three men were happy to champion a bill that was so close to their own personal interests. We had bipartisan champions in the House as well, including Representative Tony Coelho (D-CA), Representative Hamilton Fish IV (R-NY), and Representative Steny Hoyer (D-MD).

This was an incredible level of bipartisanship. We had people on both sides of the aisle who were willing to champion the bill, each of whom had key seniority on committees, which was critical in getting the bill passed. It became a passion project for all of us, especially as we had been working together on various disability rights issues in the years running up to the ADA. Everyone knew they were working on something that could make history.

We ended up introducing the bill to Congress in April 1988, and as a result, Congress formed a task force to gather examples of discrimination against people with disabilities. Over the next few months subcommittees from both the House and the Senate held hearings on disability rights, and individuals with disabilities traveled to DC to testify or wrote letters if they were unable to travel. Over the next two years Congress held over sixty public forums to hear about discrimination against people with disabilities. The stage was set for the next Congress.

By 1990 George H. W. Bush was president, and we had a new Congress. We'd been paying attention to the changes looming. President Bush had made it clear that disability rights issues were important to him, and we were confident in the ability of the coalition to do the work needed to get the ADA passed. With the start of the new congressional session, we really hit the ground running. We encountered a few stumbling blocks after introducing the bill to the Senate, due to the multipronged nature of disability rights. There were so many committees and subcommittees that could and would assert authority and jurisdiction over provisions of the bill that it often felt like we were taking a car apart: constantly worried that we wouldn't actually be able to put it all back together in the end. We were lucky that we had champions like Senators Harkin and Kennedy, who had seniority and status on many of the committees where the bill was debated; we knew we could rely on people like him to let us know what was going on.

The business community was also working hard behind the scenes to undermine many of the provisions of the bill that required public accommodations and employment practices. Even some state and local governments were quietly trying to undo provisions to enforce codes on municipal buildings and transportation. This was a very different kind of battle than working with the Senate committees; it was all behind the scenes, using money and influence to water down provisions. I sometimes longed for the fully transparent fights we had had on other issues; it is often easier to have a debate in the open than it is to fight more stealthy opponents. Yet despite all of these battles, the bill was introduced in May and was passed in the Senate in September. It was on to the House.

When the jurisdiction obstacles became overwhelming and when the subtle undermining of the bill's progress by the business community was obvious, we took to tactics traditionally used by civil rights movements—civil disobedience. In the spring of 1990, as we were trying to get momentum to get the bill done in Congress, we decided it was time for a little theater. On a lovely spring morning we asked members of the disability activist community to join us at the West Front of the Capitol building. We organized at the base of the long majestic white staircase that leads directly to the Capitol (the exact location where presidents are inaugurated). We informed the press that we intended to conduct a "civil disobedience rally." At nine thirty a.m. we'd gathered about 150 disability activists, mostly in wheelchairs or with assistive devices, at the bottom of the steps. A few remarks were made about the challenges of living in America with disabilities and then we told the gathered press that to illustrate the challenge all participants would attempt to enter their nation's Capitol. People got out of wheelchairs or threw down canes, crutches, and walkers and began to ascend the stairs—many on their hands and knees, crawling, pulling their way forward. The press went nuts; the Capitol Police did, too, since we had not asked for a permit for this "spontaneous demonstration." The interesting part was how awkwardly everyone was watching the challenge in real time and unfiltered. The event lasted about thirty minutes, until about half the participants had made it to the top. Those of us not living with a disability were charged with assisting the others and bringing all the wheelchairs and devices up to the top so people could safely exit the Capitol grounds. We had made the point, and we got those pictures that were worth a thousand words.

Building on this event and pushing harder for legislative action we issued a congressional challenge in June. The challenge was for members of Congress to volunteer for a day to do their jobs in a wheelchair. About twenty agreed. It was profoundly eye-opening for them to realize that you can't easily or quickly make your way from one office building to another or, worse, from the House and Senate offices to the Capitol when you can't walk. The stairs, narrow hallways, and lack of elevators, escalators, and curbs between all those structures present a maze of obstacles for people with disabilities. I had volunteered to be Senator Jim Jeffords's (R-VT) guide. My job was to allow him to try to make it through the day and to help only when he found it impossible to navigate his own way. The first vote was called around eleven a.m. that day, and Senator Jeffords left his office and headed to the Capitol. He got as far as the elevator in the basement of Russell building before realizing he couldn't get to the train to the Capitol because there was an escalator that could not accommodate his wheelchair. He attempted a few things, asked a Capitol policeman for help (who had no idea which way was accessible), and gave up. I was there to help. I wheeled him back to the elevators and proceeded to take him through two Senate office buildings to Hart, where the elevators actually land on the same level as the train. This took fifteen minutes—and votes are rarely held open for more than twenty minutes. He seemed relieved to get in the train and head to the Capitol building—a three-minute ride. Getting off in the basement of the Capitol presented the next challenge. There is no access to the Capitol elevators from the train, except up an escalator. No go! He was going to miss this vote. We had arranged that if needed, we'd speed up the process. I took over, wheeling Senator Jeffords down the narrow, dark, dank halls. Access to the Senate floor from the basement required a single path through the kitchens and trash areas to a service elevator. The look on Senator Jeffords's face as I wheeled him through the kitchen, over spoiled milk on the floor and trashed food waste, was priceless. He made it to the Senate chamber and took his vote. Coming out of the chamber, he said, "Do we have to do that again to get back?" "Yes, Senator," I said. "It is the only way for people with disabilities to access this building." He got the point.

———————

The bill took much longer to go through the House than it had the Senate. It was presented to four different committees, each of which ended up proposing amendments. Coalition members worked ceaselessly, meeting with representatives and their constituents to emphasize the importance of the bill. It was during these stressful months that we really started to encounter some backlash from the more conservative members of the House. First to be attacked was the inclusion of people with mental illness in the bill. We made it through that eventually with the help of some excellent lawyers from the Mental Health Law Project, but the second attack felt much more personal. Representative Dannemeyer proposed an amendment that would prevent the bill from protecting people who had contagious or sexually transmitted diseases, including AIDS. Dannemeyer had always been outspoken in his disdain for homosexuality and explicitly stated that his amendment was not meant to punish people who had AIDS as a result of a blood transfusion, but would exclude only homosexuals and drug addicts. Things were getting tense.

Dannemeyer's amendment didn't pass, but shortly afterward Representative Chapman, a Democrat from Texas, proposed a new amendment, which took us by surprise. Chapman's amendment stated that employers could, without penalty, reassign employees with infections or communicable diseases to a job that did not involve food handling. Chapman's amendment was also aimed specifically at people with AIDS, and he had the backing of the powerful National Restaurant Association. We would have never predicted such opposition would come from a Democrat. A bull's-eye was on my back. As chair of the Lobby Task Force for the ADA coalition, my job was to take all the disability groups up on the Hill to lobby every week. I mapped the targets, crafted the message, assembled the packets and one-pagers, counted votes, gathered intel, and plotted committee processes. All the while I was still working for AIDS Action Council as its policy director, and my own organization and constituency were the ones directly threatened by the Chapman amendment. Chapman had singled out "my" disease/disability for exclusion, not any others.

We didn't get lucky this time—Chapman's amendment passed. Our entire strategy for the bill was to pass the bill in one chamber and then pass the exact same bill in the other—avoiding a conference to reconcile two versions and expediting the bill to the White House for the president to sign. Our strategy was now in jeopardy, my constituents were in peril, and my leadership of the ADA coalition was potentially in question.

The Chapman amendment smelled to me of cheap politics; it seemed just an alarmist issue raised to cause contention and stop the bill in its tracks. But we had a great team of people with legal backgrounds working in the coalition, and they recognized that it was much more serious. If the bill passed with the Chapman amendment, it would have undermined the rational basis for disability coverage. Ralph Neas made the case that a major breech in Congress's commitment to disabilities would be an open door for litigation for years to come. The bill would be critically weakened, and our opponents would be able to bring constitutional challenges. Chai Feldblum made particular note that the Chapman amendment was seriously flawed in its drafting—it covered only "food handlers" but lacked any public health justification why that particular job created risk for the general public. Fear, Chai said, could not be a reason to deny a particular person with a disability the right to work and public accommodation. If the Congress codified such an irrational standard, then all civil rights statutes could be victim to such a standard. The amendment was a poison pill that would be delivered to the Supreme Court and would have resulted in the total breakdown of the act. It became obvious that we could not let the act go through with the Chapman amendment.

This was when the divisions in the disability rights movement really came to the fore, and I was in the middle of it. I was in the awful situation of being the lobby chair on behalf of the entire committee while my particular community was threatening the status of the entire bill. Some of the people in the disability rights movement were ready to write people with AIDS out of the ADA. They had worked for so many years to get civil rights protections, and they were so close—it seemed logical to them that if we had to be sacrificed, they were willing to do it. I knew this was not the way to proceed, and Pat Wright backed me up, saying she did not think dumping the AIDS community was wise legally or politically. Thankfully that option was off the table, but we now had to figure out what our other options were.

We considered passing a different version of the House bill (sans Chapman) in the Senate, but that would have forced a conference between the House and Senate. The House and Senate have to pass the exact same version of the other's bill, or it has to go to conference to negotiate the differences. Only one version passed by both the House and Senate can proceed to the White House for the president's signature. When the House passed the ADA with the Chapman amendment in place through to its final version, we were faced with either accepting it in the Senate or rejecting it and possibly going into a conference that could swallow the bill (by holding it until Congress recessed, thereby killing it).

We considered passing the House version and attempting a bill in the next Congress to amend the ADA by stripping Chapman, but we rejected that as unlikely and a major blow to the AIDS community that would have wider repercussions (remember, Ryan White was rapidly moving at the same time behind the ADA). Finally we considered our last option: bring the ADA to the Senate, amend it by stripping Chapman, and then return it to the House. The key to the strategy was a single simple equation: Did we have the votes we needed to prevail in the Senate? Did we have fifty-one votes, enough to pass a motion to strike Chapman, and would we then have sixty votes if the effect of stripping Chapman brought a filibuster from Helms and the right wing? If we prevailed in the Senate, would the House take offense and simply reject our amendment by the same vote they accepted Chapman to begin with? This was a very stressful time. Even once everyone in the coalition agreed to pull together, we didn't know if we would have enough votes to get the bill through.

That's how I found myself sitting in Kennedy's hideaway in the Senate. Senator Kennedy started by very directly stating that the choices here were grave and that it was his intention to let the leadership of the disability community decide on the course of action. He did warn that failure might place the ADA out of reach for at least the rest of the Congress and possibly longer. Senator Harkin spoke next; he affirmed Senator Kennedy's intention but layered on his personal passion for the bill, its landmark possibilities, its impact on his own brother, and the great pressure he was feeling from all of the disability groups who were counting on him to deliver on this bill. He also noted that he was up for reelection in Iowa in November, and he was counting on the ADA to help him become the first Democratic senator from Iowa to serve for more than one term. If we didn't pass the bill now, it was entirely possible that we would lose one of our champions.

Next, the room turned to me. I said we had taken a very fast whip count of our support in the Senate for striking Chapman (we had done it that afternoon by a mad flurry of phone calls). I was very confident we had the fifty-one votes to win an up/down on striking Chapman. I hesitated, and then reluctantly told the group that we were likely short four votes of the sixty we would need to end a filibuster. Simply put, I knew I had fifty-six solid supporters for an ADA that included people with AIDS/HIV, but I could not say with certainty that I had sixty. After my statement there was silence from the group. It was probably just for a minute, but to me it felt like hours. Nearly all of us were frustrated to have been placed in such an awful position.

Senator Kennedy finally broke the silence, noting that if we brought the bill to the floor without a clear strategy to manage this problem, we would invite its total demise. He went on to say that the decision must be clear and must be acceptable to the disability community. Then he turned to me again: "Is there anything you think you could do to secure those four votes?" Thankfully, we were prepared for that question, and we had an idea. I began by saying, "Senator Orrin Hatch is the Republican co-sponsor of Ryan White. We've been working closely with him and with good results. The staff gets along well, the community has found an unusual but reliable partner, and he values the collaboration with Senator Kennedy. We think if we can get Hatch to support or even offer the amendment to strike Chapman that we could pick up the swing votes that were mainly on the Republican side." The problem was we'd only be able to negotiate this support from Hatch after the bill began consideration on the floor. If the Hatch strategy failed, the bill would either pass with Chapman in it or it would be sent back to the committee for reconsideration (likely killing it for the remainder of the Congress). This was a very high-risk strategy, but we had no other choice.

I was in the hot seat—my own organization's issue was the one that was threatening to take the ADA down, and people from both the left and the right were questioning my competency and capacity to lead. Now the big decision was up to me. The trust Kennedy was placing in me felt immense— how did he know I would make the right decision? We had all worked so hard, and now with one false step we could completely lose the bill. I'll never forget the feeling of leaving the Senate that night after deciding to strip the Chapman amendment from the House bill. I had just made a huge decision that would shape the future of the ADA.

The next morning, Michael Iskowitz and Caroline Osolinik from Senator Kennedy's staff, Chai Feldblum, and I had a meeting with Senator Hatch's top staff and explained to them that there was no rational or public health basis for the Chapman amendment. People with AIDS were not going to cause any harm if they worked with food. The staff agreed to take the request to the senator, who was already on the floor. We all walked over together, and then we waited in the anteroom while they went to the cloakroom to talk with the senator. He came out to meet with us, and after we made our case he said he needed to think about it and make a few calls to see what "the other side" might say. I'm not sure if he really believed us in that moment, but he went back into the cloakroom and started making phone calls. He called both Chapman and the National Restaurant Association and asked them what the public health basis was for the amendment. The Restaurant Association basically said they just thought the ADA will be bad for business, but there was no public health rationale. They were worried that if word got out that restaurants were employing people with AIDS, no one would come to eat at those businesses. It was a decision based on stereotypes and fear, not one based on facts. Chapman basically admitted to doing it only at the behest of the National Restaurant Association—a significant supporter with PAC money and other in-kind donations to his campaign.

After having those conversations, Hatch came back out to talk to us and offered a compromise. While he understood there was no public health basis for the AIDS portion of the amendment, he wanted to create a related amendment based on scientific facts. This would come to be known as the exceptions amendment. He wanted to soften the strike with allowances for employers to reassign employees with a communicable disease to jobs that did not require food handling, but only if the disease was scientifically considered communicable—that is, transmitted through air and proximity. Hatch also wanted a section that specified that people with a disease that could actually be considered harmful to others would not be covered by the ADA.

We ended up going through the *Diagnostic and Statistical Manual of Mental Disorders* looking for things that were classified as a disease that could actually be harmful to other individuals—things like necrophilia or pedophilia. It was an incredibly bizarre situation, especially after the stress of the night before, but if you read the ADA, there are actually some specific diagnoses listed that are not covered. So we did end up with a public health provision, but one that was based on scientific fact and didn't exclude people with AIDS or people who had mental illnesses. As a result, we had an amendment to strike Chapman and replace it with the Hatch proposal and ended up with the numbers we needed. Hatch got on board and brought a few other Republicans with him. We had succeeded, but the battle was not yet won. Since we had changed the bill it had to be brought back to the House for final approval. After a lot of chaos and some running back and forth between the Senate and the House, we were finally successful. We had a bill to present to the president.

In the end, decades of work came down to a total sprint. The actual legislative effort took two and a half years. I don't think there had ever been anything like it before—that much concerted legislative effort being successful so quickly. That's part of what I love about the story of the ADA: our coalition was able to achieve something historic despite having absolutely no independent funding. This coalition was unique for many reasons, but one of them was the fact that all of its resources were donated—in kind, mostly. We had no formal organizational home; we had no independent operating budget. Leaders of the coalition were expected to bring themselves, their time, and all the organizational resources they could muster to the table for collective action. For that reason I seriously contemplated calling this chapter "Cheaper by the Dozens" or "Many Hands Make Light Work." One of these phrases is the slightly modified title of a Lucille Ball movie from the 1970s (a favorite of mine); the other was an expression my grandfather liked to use when rousing his grandchildren to a particular project he'd decided to tackle. Joking aside, both express the same value or idea for why coalitions matter in creating effective change: when you can bring together resources from multiple sources you have more to work with. That's how the ADA coalition was conceived and managed, and that's why it was so successful. Being a part of this unique coalition has had a huge impact on me—any time a job requires me to form a coalition, I look back at the ADA for inspiration.

Second View: Pat Wright

The most important aspect of successfully enacting a piece of legislation is to know when to hold 'em and when to fold 'em: you have to know when to

---

compromise, and when to hold out for a better deal. To do that successfully, you need to always do your homework, which will allow you to anticipate forces that could arise and how they would align themselves in relation to a controversial issue. Constantly gather background information on members of Congress that could be used whenever needed. Learn how to count votes. Develop strategies with numerous layers and backup positions. Create several routes of access to top decision makers and persons of influence in Congress, the White House, and outside of government. Develop knowledge of both the overall political landscape and the many ongoing agendas that operate within it. And that's the easy part. Holding the coalition together, well...that's another story. There is no easy way.

Developing principles for your coalition at the start of the legislative process is critical. It is the only way to keep a disparate group of people who all have different agendas together. Each amendment presented by the coalition should be measured against the principles, and no amendment should be accepted that violates the principles. If you are able to clearly stand by your principles, you can keep the process from being derailed. At one point during the legislative process of the ADA a faction within the coalition attempted to have me removed by arguing to congressional members that I was not representing their interests. Another time late in the process, the same group went to the White House and tried to pitch an amendment that was different from what the civil rights community and disability community had agreed to. However, by sticking to our principles throughout the process, the trust that we had developed with the White House and congressional members was so strong that both attempts to break up our group and our bill were dismissed. Using the principles, all my actions were tested against the allegations.

However, late in the final passage, the Chapman amendment became a great example of how even the best strategy can go awry even if you have backup plans. The Chapman amendment was introduced and passed on the House side. If left in the final bill, this amendment would have violated a primary principle that held the coalition together.

Our only hope was to remove the amendment and to invoke a core principle of all for one and one for all. We took the position that we would let the bill die before allowing one group (in this case, people with HIV/AIDS) to be excluded from its coverage. We had an emergency meeting at the White House with C. Boyden Gray, counsel to President Bush. Bob Williams, a leader in the disability rights community, who has cerebral palsy, summed up the disability community's feeling about the amendment by spelling out on his talking board: "It ain't civil and it ain't right." My leadership and the coalition were never fully tested as to whether we would actually ask the leadership to pull the bill, because after much lobbying before conference an agreement was worked out that turned the amendment into a study and avoided excluding people with HIV/AIDS from the bill.

Although the defeat of that amendment will be viewed as a success in public policy circles, the process took a significant personal toll: Some members of the AIDS lobbying community thought that an all-or-nothing stance was too risky and wanted to offer a compromise amendment. I argued against their amendment; after collecting all the data and counting my votes I knew that it would be close, but I made a decision and recommended to Senators Kennedy and Harkin that we should go for it. This is the part of coalition work that takes guts, the ability to stand alone when even your friends are not sure and to be willing to take the heat. During that process I lost some of my friends but gained some admirers. In situations like these your career and reputation are on the line. There will always be people within the coalition who don't agree with you, so the answer is that you must believe in yourself. That is the price you pay to head a coalition. In the final analysis, determining when to hold out and when to compromise is an art more than a science. Oh, and one more thing: never look back.

TAKEAWAYS

My time working on the ADA taught me a lot about coalitions and how they can and should function. If you are thinking about forming a coalition, there are a few things I recommend that you keep in mind.

First, coalitions function best when there is a specific product or goal everyone is committed to achieving through mutual effort.

The goal of the ADA coalition was evident right from the start. We were working to provide civil rights to all people with disabilities, even marginalized groups like people with mental illnesses or AIDS. Sticking to this goal wasn't easy, but we always knew where we were headed. Coalitions that are formed without a specific product or goal end up cycling endlessly. There are meetings and committees and conversations, but nothing actually results in any action.

Coalitions with a goal are committed to achieving results, which makes for a tighter group. There are no free rides: if you are going to be a part of the effort, you have to be willing to bring something to the table. Each of us in the ADA coalition had to be willing to take time away from our own organizations to work on ADA efforts. Every hour we spent working on the ADA was an hour we couldn't devote to our own organizations, and everyone had to be willing to make that commitment.

Second, coalitions should have a fundamental commitment to the highest common denominator.

When you are setting your goals for a coalition, it is important to make sure that you are committing your efforts to the highest common denominator. This is often counterintuitive and countercultural for many in the "do good" space. The principal value for many nonprofit groups is consensus, but I firmly believe that you cannot let consensus cost you your goal. If you make too many compromises, you can lose sight of your goal, and in the end, winning becomes meaningless. Having this commitment to the highest common denominator may mean that certain members have to leave a coalition, but in my experience people don't want to leave the pack. People are more afraid of leaving the group than they are of a bolder policy, strategy, or tactic. You can use this to your advantage to keep the commitments high. When we held the line on the Chapman amendment, everyone else eventually fell into place.

Third, in order for an in-kind coalition to succeed, its leadership must take personal and organizational responsibility for achieving the goals of the group.

This is how you hold it all together for the long run. Forming a coalition means that there will always have to be some minor internal compromises—this is necessary to keep everyone working together. Also necessary is a sense of mutuality: coalition members have to be willing to give credit to others and share the work of the group.

In order to keep all of these moving parts together, you need a strong leader who is fiercely dedicated to the goal. In the ADA coalition we had General Pat, and her ability to hold the line during the Chapman amendment crisis is what really allowed us to prevail. When there is a crisis in the coalition, you need a leader who is prepared to be stern and who knows the value of achieving the goals.

KEY QUOTES AND LESSONS

- Never surprise anyone in your coalition. Make sure you are all on the same page.
- A commitment to achieving results means there are no free rides. If you participate in the effort, you have to commit yourself and bring your resources.
- No rights without remedies. You can't assert a right to accessibility unless you can enforce the standards. Legislation is hard work; don't allow it to become a

resolution—pretty on paper but without teeth and real change.

- Pay attention to the opposition—even if you can't see them. The National Restaurant Association came out of nowhere and surprised us, but in the end we also knew they didn't have facts, just fear. When we turned that against them, we won the day.

THE THREE P 'S FOR ADA

Policy: The ADA was the most significant piece of civil rights legislation since the Voting Rights Act of 1968, sweeping and far reaching, helping a new class of Americans who experienced discrimination but had no legal redress. The broad definition of disability was bold and aggressive, and the remedies it sought reached into every aspect of American society. This was historic policy in every sense of the word.

Politics: The disability community didn't have the political muscle of the civil rights groups that had come before them. African Americans had decades of struggle with leaders and disruption and attention. Women had taken political power to a new level in the 1970s and asserted their power in numbers. People with disabilities had none of these political resources or assets. Winning took a coalition effort of unparalleled proportion—big enough to create the politics to win. The coalition brought together groups that had never worked together before. It was risky but worth it.

Press: We tried to localize the press as much as we could. We targeted editorial boards in local papers and used local disability advocates to seek the support of media elites. The more localized we pushed the issue, the more charitable its intent and political framework became. This helped neutralize the business community before they could mount their more selfish opposition. We did find ourselves stuck at one point and orchestrated a civil disobedience event on the steps of the Capitol—where people in wheelchairs and with canes discarded their assistive devices and crawled up the steps of the Capitol on the West Front. It was very dramatic and got a ton of press coverage. You do need some stagecraft to get press attention.

CHAPTER 4

Combating Human Trafficking

"One person's vision can catalyze change"

IN 2007, *Amazing Grace* was released on the big screen. Months before it hit the theaters, I watched the movie at an advance showing. In the darkened theater I felt proud, but more immediately, I felt revolted. I could now see scenes of the slave trade with my own eyes, horrifying images from history brought to life. I recall a particular scene where workers on a slave ship go belowdecks just before arriving at port, haul out dozens of bodies, and throw them overboard. All of these people had died during the long trip and remained in the cabin, their bodies decomposing until shortly before arrival at port, when workers disposed of the "expired cargo." The lack of humanity displayed in the film is striking; the injustices and utter inhumanity of slavery are driven home with a visceral punch. Then the credits fade, the screen goes black, and a message appears, a message that gives a clue as to what I was doing at that advance screening: Please call your senators and representatives and ask them to support the Wilberforce Act. The message remains on screen with the number for the US Capitol switchboard, urging you to make a difference in fighting modern-day slavery. The tie-in to the movie *Amazing Grace* was the capstone of a strategic advocacy and lobbying effort, and it would ultimately provide our group working on the issue with a large media platform, allowing us incredible success when it came to passing landmark legislation aimed at ending modern-day slavery.

Looking back on it, the whole chain of events that led to the passing of the Wilberforce Act was full of coincidences, but the path to success was also marked by the hard work of many individuals. It all started in early 2006. I was at a meeting for Hope Lab, a health-focused R&D group that aims to improve the health and well-being of adolescents and young adults. Hope Lab was founded by Pam Omidyar, the wife of eBay founder Pierre Omidyar, and my dear friend and colleague Pat Christen was the CEO. Pat and I had worked together at the San Francisco AIDS Foundation, and she invited me to meet Pam and learn about Hope Lab. After the meeting Pam stopped me and asked my opinion on a different matter: what did I think about doing some advocacy work on human trafficking and slavery? She had been funding some smaller groups across the country and wanted to talk about expanding the effort.

After thinking it over for a bit, I gave her my honest answer: I believed people just didn't think slavery was a problem anymore. In order to do any good work on the issue, you would first have to build a whole public education and awareness campaign around it. It wouldn't be enough to just advocate for new policies; you would have to create the crisis yourself, make people really aware of the issue. This would not be an easy task; it would be hard and expensive and complicated.

Pam, undeterred, invited me to a meeting with some of the groups she was currently funding. All of the groups were operating on a very micro level: they were running hotlines and working with very specific groups of people in very specific locations. They were doing good and important work, but they were not ready for a full-on lobbying effort; they were not ready to take it to DC. The resources just weren't there. They didn't have funding, they had no policy expertise, and there was little to no political sophistication among them. What did impress me was their dedication, their ability to make what seemed like an old problem very current. They had the gift of storytelling, especially two groups: Free the Slaves and Polaris. Free the Slaves had been working on the issue the longest and had written books on the subject. Polaris, while newer, had set up a trafficking hotline that allowed them to connect with real-time stories of modern-day slavery. Those stories gave them of-the-moment flavor that was very powerful and real. Such storytelling can be a very effective way to create momentum for policy solutions, but they didn't have the skills to craft that policy. My conclusion was that it was not really a movement, and it would take substantial time and resources to create one on this issue.

About three months later I was approached by a film company with a proposition that could make Pam's goals achievable. The year 2007 was to be the two-hundredth anniversary of an antislavery act that was passed in the British Parliament, and this company was making a movie about the act and the men who campaigned for it. They explained to me a little bit about the plot and the characters of the movie, and I was fascinated. The movie focused on a man named William Wilberforce, who was elected to Parliament when he was just twenty-one years old. After becoming an evangelical Christian, he became a fierce abolitionist. The Slave Trade Act of 1807 was his great achievement; it abolished the slave trade throughout the British Empire. Working with Wilberforce on the act was a man named John Newton. Newton had served on a slave ship as a young man but then also converted to evangelical Christianity and campaigned against his former employers. Newton eventually became a priest and wrote the poem that is now called "Amazing Grace," from which the movie took its title.

The movie company wanted our affiliated PR company, Venture Communications, to create a PR campaign that would excite activists to see the movie and stir interest in the issue. The Sheridan Group was brought in to design a way to capture moviegoers into a grassroots network in order to take some action on the issue of modern-day slavery. The movie company wanted buzz and a constituency to increase ticket sales, but they were also willing to extend that reach to advocacy—a very smart and effective idea. The movie would create a teachable moment, a way to raise awareness of a historical problem, and we could then capture informed and moved moviegoers and attempt to enlist them in our advocacy network. Right away, I knew this could be a perfect moment—the film would create the public education that I had told Pam we were lacking. If people were moved by the story they had seen, we could inform them that slavery was still an issue in the modern world and that they could help end the problem by contacting members of Congress. Now I was really intrigued; I loved the idea of taking on something that was so important but totally lacking in public or political recognition. We could bring people along from information to action and then to activism. These kinds of opportunities are rare, but I saw similarities to the beginning of my work with the AIDS lobby, and I wanted to prove we could build another transformational movement.

———

Before I could go back to Pam and really get the project started, I needed to do some research myself to try to understand the full scope of the issue. I had learned a little from my meetings with Pam's various groups, but I needed a deeper understanding of the issue if I was going to mobilize an advocacy campaign, and I needed a hook, line, and sinker combination to really get the process started.

Our research discovered some nascent work in policy on this issue—in 2000, the Trafficking Victims Protection Act

(TVPA) had been passed with bipartisan support. The TVPA required, among other things, that the United States produce an annual report on the human rights practices and extent of human trafficking in foreign countries. Additionally, the TVPA authorized protection for immigrants who were victims of severe trafficking and created the T visa. The T visa allows victims of trafficking to remain in the United States while they assist in the investigation and prosecution of human trafficking cases. Victims may apply for permanent residency after their T visa has expired. The bill promoted protection and assistance for victims of trafficking both in the United States and around the world, and contained the authority for the Department of State to set up an office on human trafficking and slavery. The office had begun to create policy and regulations giving the US government power to monitor the extent of the problem worldwide and even look into sanctions for those countries at the forefront of the problem.

We also discovered that the authority for this office technically expired in 2007 and required reauthorization by Congress. Here was our hook: Congress would rewrite and pass this bill in honor of the Wilberforce anniversary, and we'd use the bill as the focus of the grassroots network we had been hired to develop. The "line" followed immediately: we would have people ask their members of Congress to support the act after they had watched the movie. Now we needed the sinker—an effective campaign that would absorb the grassroots into a DC-based lobbying effort. Effective advocacy work requires that you give people a clear request that they can make: for instance, "Tell your members of Congress to pass this bill." This is a concrete action people can take, as opposed to a limp message like "Tell your members of Congress you're worried about human trafficking and slavery."

Armed with a better idea of the overall scale of the issue, I went back to Pam with the resources of the film company behind me and asked her to underwrite the sinker part of our plan: a coalition. Pam decided that Humanity United, a foundation Pam had started to find solutions to global atrocities like genocide and slavery, would handle our contract. Pam introduced me to Randy Newcomb, who was the CEO of HU, and so it was HU that became our client—they agreed to sponsor a coalition of provider groups, if we could bring them all together.

———————

Clearly our first step was to contact all the different organizations Pam had been funding on the issue. They were a pretty diverse group, some of which were highly religious, and some of which were completely secular. They had been working in different areas of the country and all around the world, focusing on different specific groups of people, and they didn't know each other well at all. In the rare case where they did know one another, there was a simmering animosity that you'll find with organizations that are in coopetition with each other. The smaller the movement and the budget, the fiercer this coopetition can be (more on coopetition a little later). Yet despite their differences, we were able to get them all to agree on one thing: the current policies were just not doing what needed to be done, and this was the moment to try to change that. Additionally, Pam was the biggest funder around on this issue. If she wanted them to work on policy in coalition, they were in no position to argue or object. Most were willing and excited to begin this level of work.

Our idea was to sit down with Pam's grassroots organizations and do a rewrite of the TVPA that would really focus on the current state of the problem of slavery and human trafficking. We wanted to get the opinions of the people on the ground and the people actually doing the work to combat these problems, and then transform those opinions into a series of amendments that we could bring to Congress to get the bill reauthorized. This is a habit I developed during my time with the AIDS lobby, and one that has served me well to this day: write policy only after you've seen or been given witness to a problem and its solution from as close to it as you can get. It soon became evident that our goal was to get the government to fund programs that actually assisted in solving the problems experienced by victims, as well as strengthening sanctions and punishments for offenders.

Now we had a plan, and we had the money to get the plan started, but we soon ran into another issue. None of the people in Pam's groups had any experience with advocacy. They didn't know how the process worked, and they didn't know how to use it to their benefit. We didn't have the type of senior-level talent that you usually need to run an advocacy campaign like this, but I knew there was a way to piece it together. If we could attract a few knowledgeable people to our cause, we could harness the energy of the more inexperienced people and really make some changes.

At that point there weren't really many people working on the issue of trafficking at a macro level. Pam was doing her best, but she was a philanthropist, not a political activist. The first person who came to my mind was Melanne Verveer. She had been chief of staff for Hillary Clinton during Bill Clinton's administration and had overseen Clinton's global initiatives on women's rights. She had been instrumental in getting the TVPA passed in 2000 and was a co-founder of Vital Voices Global Partnership, an NGO that focused on supporting women leaders and fighting human rights abuses around the world. Human trafficking is particularly an issue for women and girls, and so Melanne had become very invested in the issue; I knew we needed her on our team. Melanne was already familiar with some of the program providers so we were able to capitalize on her credibility. After getting Melanne on board, we approached Holly Burkhalter, a human rights expert nominated by President Bill Clinton and confirmed by the US Senate to serve on the board of directors of the US Institute of Peace, who also had experience lobbying. Holly would prove to be an incredible asset; she was really down in the trenches, and in tough moments she was able to convince her colleagues to give us the benefit of the doubt and press on. These two women were essential in our efforts to convince the other players that joining our coalition would be to their benefit. We slowly started to present the idea of the coalition to the inexperienced and somewhat skeptical remaining groups, and they eventually agreed to join us.

———————

Oddly enough, we soon began attracting a wide variety of celebrities to our cause as well. Through my previous experiences with Bono, I knew the power celebrities could bring to a cause, so I welcomed them into our odd little group. Singer Ricky Martin was one of the first people interested in our coalition. I didn't know it at the time, but he had established a foundation that worked to denounce and expose human trafficking, with a special emphasis on children and youth in Latin America. This was a cause close to his heart: in 2002 on a trip to India he came face-to-face with children who were being sold into prostitution. He had already testified in front of Congress once about the existence of modern slavery, and I was happy to have him add some star power to our cause. Ricky was our star witness at the hearings for the act, and he also brought an invaluable amount of press to our overall campaign.

The night before the hearing I went to the Park Hyatt hotel to brief Ricky on the substance of the bill and to practice the testimony. He was warm and engaged and seriously committed to this issue, but like I always did with Bono, I wanted to be sure he was prepared for some of the downsides of standing up on issues like this. Michael Jackson was in the news at that particular moment for his exploits with children that bordered on molestation, or at the very least were highly inappropriate. I warned Ricky that the underbelly of this issue, especially in regard to sex trafficking of young girls, could attract a creep factor to the tone of questions or comments he may receive. He looked genuinely horrified, like he didn't fully understand what I meant. We discussed it for a few minutes and then I finally said, "You have to be totally comfortable in your own skin on these matters. You can't appear to be ambivalent on the issues and the gravity of them. If someone were to ask, 'Why does a famous singer care so much about these girls?' you'll need a simple, straightforward response." There were rumors that Ricky was gay, but he had not yet come out publicly, and his staff and agent weren't prepared to raise those questions or inadvertently trip him into an area he wasn't ready to talk about. I was aware of this and wanted to be sure we had minimally prepared him if motives or his personal life were brought up. We crafted our response based on his experience in India and the horror he felt and saw in those children's eyes. The prepared answer was pretty simple: *I've been around long enough and lived in the real world. I know victims when I see them. I've seen bullying, abuse, and victimization. I can recognize terror in an innocent person's eyes. When you see it, you know it, and it is impossible for a moral person to turn away.* He never needed to use the answer, but he had it. And it worked. Talking obliquely with a celebrity about his or her own motivations and personal life can be tricky and uncomfortable, but in the end it's your job to be sure your allies and advocates are prepared.

Two other celebrities ended up working with us to develop public support for the reauthorization: American actress

Daryl Hannah and English actress Julia Ormond also gave us immense support. Daryl had made a documentary about sexual slavery in which she went to brothels in Southeast Asia in disguise, and Julia had founded the Alliance to Stop Slavery and End Trafficking after witnessing trafficking in Eastern Europe in the 1990s. While neither woman did any day-to-day work with the coalition, they were involved in some very important strategic moments: Hill meetings, press interviews, and outreach.

Daryl Hannah surprised us all in an interview she was doing at our behest when she revealed her own personal story: as a young actress she had been seduced into a human trafficking ring, and then was able to escape. She and three other friends trying to make it in LA were invited to a party in Las Vegas all expenses paid: car, hotel suite, food, drinks. After the weekend ended they were asked if they wanted to go to an audition at a smaller hotel outside of town. Daryl and her friends thought it was their big break. Upon arrival, they were locked in the hotel room. Their host from the party arrived to inform them that they'd piled up a $25,000 bill in Vegas and they'd have to work it off before he'd let them go. When the man left the room, the women figured out an escape: using nail files and things in their makeup kits they cut the screen in the bathroom window and escaped. They ran to a nearby gas station and called the police.

We benefited greatly from the work those two women did to help promote our campaign.

We had created a true hodgepodge of a coalition, but it was time to get down to work. The movie already had a release date, and if we were going to be able to use their money and outreach, we had to be ready with the bill in time. We had a sixteen-month window in which we needed to get all of this done, and we needed every second of it. Sometimes it felt like we were still putting the wings on the plane as it was taking off.

When it came time to actually write the amendments to the bill, we started to discover some complications in the organization of our coalition. Pam had been working with a variety of different groups, and they had never had to work together before. It was one of our operating principles that every member of the group was to be a co-equal partner, regardless of their past relationships with HU, but that didn't automatically mean that everyone was united. This can be one of the flaws in single-funded coalitions: the members are totally subject to the funder's decisions. In this case, Pam made it clear that she would put more resources behind any program that embraced advocacy. Suddenly all these separate micro groups had to work together and start to think at a macro level.

The diversity of the groups led to some interesting conflicts, especially around the issues of sex trafficking. Many of the religious groups were quite evangelical, and sex trafficking was a huge focus for them. We often found ourselves reminding those groups that labor trafficking was also a huge issue and trying to keep them from focusing entirely on one aspect of the issue. Further complicating things was the fact

that some of the other groups were actively fighting to legal-
ize prostitution. A key player at the Sheridan Group in all
of this was Sara Guderyahn, a young staff member who had
joined us after a very successful internship. Sara was referred
by my best friend, who had employed her as a babysitter for
my godchildren. Yes, Washington is a small world, and a
humble job can sometimes lead to big things.

Sara had just completed her graduate degree in political
affairs at American University. Young, bright, and enthusiastic, she worked hard and stayed with projects and tasks until
she got them to completion. She had the traits of a great progressive lobbyist and needed a chance to show them off and
build some experience. At the Sheridan Group, she was put
under the watchful mentorship of Nancy Stetson, a senior-
level advisor for foreign affairs and international development. Nancy was old-school—tough, disciplined, unyielding
in excellence, and encyclopedic on all things related to policy and international development. They were an amazing
team paired with an amazing coalition, but there was little
commonality among any of the groups. That tension created
the energy and the vibrancy that drove this effort to success.
Sara, her first time in the jump seat, did a really fantastic job
of putting in the wing bolts of the plane as we were taking
flight, to harken back to that airplane theory of change and
getting the left and right wing to work together.

Getting everyone to work together was good practice for
what we would face when we got into the legislative process.
Legislating is by definition an act of compromise; it is a
fatal error to think you can use the legislative process to

get 100 percent of what you want. In this case the hard and sometimes frustrating moments of this coalition yielded compromises that directly benefited our lobbying on Capitol Hill. When right-wing members met with religious groups, they got a bill that came with the endorsements of groups they trusted, and the same was true on the progressive side. While it was hard work keeping things amicable, it truly paid off down the line.

Despite these hurdles, all of the groups of the coalition were composed of people who cared deeply about the cause, and that led to some truly inspiring moments. As we began to educate them about advocacy and policy, things started to come together, and everyone really pitched in. We asked each of the program providers to give us data and stories. When we expanded the reach of the act to new areas (such as the diplomatic corps) or went deeper on program challenges (like immigration and law enforcement undermining victims who wanted to come forward), we needed solid examples of how these programs and services would do better with the amended provisions and what the ill effects of the current law were doing to the lives of real people.

I knew we were working with some dedicated people, but I remember one moment when it became incredibly clear how much effort some of the younger members were putting into the process. I was talking to some of the members of Polaris, an organization dedicated to working directly with victims, and they mentioned that they had spent their Saturday night working on an amendment while simultaneously fielding calls from their trafficking hotline. They were the first stop for many victims—the stories were fresh and raw and tragic, and they reminded us of why we were writing the bill. That combination of on-the-ground work and policy writing was what made this coalition so powerful; they may not have known much about policy when the coalition was first started, but they were completely committed to the cause. Great policy is written when it starts and stays close to the programs and people who are doing the most effective work to solve the problem. Often there is too much distance, perhaps even no connection, between advocates who write policy and program providers who serve real people. We had no such issue, and it showed in the quality of policy work we were able to produce.

It meant more than a few late nights, but we were able to hit our deadline; by the time *Amazing Grace* was being released in theaters, we had presented our bill to Congress. We were able to ask moviegoers to write to their senators and representatives and support our bill by name: the William Wilberforce Trafficking Victims Protection Reauthorization Act. The coalition had come up with twenty-six amendments to the original bill—twenty-six places where things could be improved to really focus on the issue at hand.

When I first started looking into the issue, I had been told by many groups that the original TVPA had promised them $15 million, and they didn't know where it had gone. We discovered that a lot of that money had just never been appropriated, and so they hadn't been able to use it. Apparently the advocates for the original bill didn't understand that authorizations were just purchase orders and that an entirely separate process is needed to actually get the money. Once you have a bill that authorizes a program or service, you then need to go through another process to get the cash, and you have to go through the process every single year in order to renew your funding. The previous effort didn't know they needed to take the second step, and so they had never gotten any money. This is a common but fatal error; just because the bill passed doesn't mean you have won the fight. We wanted to address that issue in the WWA and make sure that the previous programs were reauthorized and actually received their money. Many of our amendments focused on that aspect—the TVPA had some great ideas about how to address the issue of human trafficking, but there were some major gaps that needed to be filled. Looking back, I can identify three of those amendments that I think really made some of the most important changes to the original TVPA.

One of the most important things we heard from our coalition members was that there was a real lack of integration. Different groups collected different data, and there was no way to see the bigger picture. It seemed inconceivable that we were trying to solve such a global issue without sharing information. We wrote up an amendment to specifically target this issue: the WWA requires the creation of an integrated database that contains data from all of the federal agencies involved in combating human trafficking. Having this massive database would allow for an analysis of global patterns in human trafficking as well as the identification of issues as they emerged.

Another important change we wanted to make to the TVPA was to address the issue of labor recruiters who recruit foreign laborers to work in the United States under false pretenses. We heard many stories from coalition members of people who had been recruited to work in the United States and did not realize that they would be working under forced labor conditions. The TVPA did not provide the ability to prosecute these recruiters for their exploitative actions, and so we wrote an amendment for the WWA that clearly designated this as a crime, punishable by up to five years of imprisonment.

The third important amendment related to how we could help US citizens who were victims of trafficking. This amendment ensured that when programs to help US citizen trafficking victims were created, the government would consult with NGOs like our coalition members to help determine what kinds of services the victims might need. These programs would allow for communication between different assistance providers so that victims could easily be referred to services they might need. For example, victims might need shelter and also trauma counseling. These new programs would allow them to get the help they needed.

———

By the time President Bush signed our act into law on December 23, 2008, twenty-five and a half of our amendments were still intact. You may be curious about the half.

Well, our twenty-sixth amendment attempted to add two new layers into consequences for members of the diplomatic corps found engaging in trafficking behavior: criminal consequences here in the US, and sanctions against their home nation, revoking certain privileges extended by the US while they are residing here. The State Department hated the second prong, as it was difficult to enforce and carried the potential for retaliatory actions by other nations against US diplomats. We conceded that half of the enforcement provision, but kept the other half. The combination of young, inexperienced, passionate people and senior-level experts had paid off. Our coalition had had an incredible impact on the new law, and as a result it extended greater protections to human trafficking victims in the US and abroad, and provided US officials with additional tools to help ensure that traffickers were brought to justice. We had come a long way from my first conversation with Pam, and thanks to the publicity provided by the movie studio, we had brought an issue from the sidelines to the forefront of public knowledge. Great timing, hard work, and some luck paid off in the form of generating a groundswell of support to radically improve a historic bill.

Second View: Sara Guderyahn

While being ushered through the White House to the West Wing, I caught a glimpse out the window of the visitors staring through the perimeter fence. I imagined I saw my twelve-year-old self, fanny pack fastened around my waist, gripping the bars and straining for a glimpse of the important work going on inside, excitedly announcing to my parents that I was going to be in there one day, helping the country. It was a surreal, full-circle moment for a twenty-six-year-old just starting a career in advocacy.

Our group of fifteen advocates was led to the Roosevelt Room to wait for the bill-signing ceremony. I looked around the table and reflected on the journey that led to this moment.

Just two years ago, almost to the day, I had walked down the hall to my desk after a meeting with Tom, president of the Sheridan Group. As a new and junior employee, that was not a regular occurrence. I had been handed an opportunity (Tom referred to it as a sink-or-swim moment) to lead on a report for Free the Slaves. My charge was to find out everything I could about the group's work and then to launch and lead a coalition of service providers focused on developing a policy agenda to end modern-day slavery. While I had studied international policy as an undergraduate at American University, what I knew about human trafficking could fill exactly one page of a notebook.

I went back to my desk and sat down. My first

thought was, *No way I can do this.* I gave myself exactly five minutes to panic, and then I picked up the phone and called a friend who was working on the Senate Foreign Relations Committee. "I'm coming over, and I need to know everything you know about human trafficking and what the United States is doing to end it." That began the first of seventy-six interviews over the next sixty days. I talked to staff on Capitol Hill, service providers in the United States and around the world, and survivors of human trafficking.

This was the first of many times I found myself on my learning edge—one side of the edge made me want to run to Tom and beg him to have someone else take on this work, and on the other side I found myself charging forward, not knowing when I was in way over my head. One moment was the night before a key coalition meeting when it seemed everyone was at odds over one or more policy recommendations. I got calls from members threatening to leave the coalition and withdraw support from the bill. I recognized it was a moment to leverage strategic expertise. Tom was able to help me navigate an incredibly tough and anxious coalition meeting the next day, and my key takeaway was that it was okay to ask for help and support.

But most challenges to pass this legislation came

directly from Capitol Hill. In fact, it seemed likely from the very start it would be an uphill climb. It was 2008, and just as we made it through committee, one of the chief sponsors, Joe Biden, accepted the nomination for vice president. Overnight we lost one of our biggest and most strategic champions. Members only wanted to talk about economic recovery or election strategies. While we made it past committee markup, we could not get the floor time to pass the legislation. And then, a Hail Mary opportunity presented itself—ironically interconnected with the thing that for months we were competing with—the bailout of the auto industry.

Postelection, Congress was talking about a legislative session expressly to consider and pass the auto bailout plan. Our bill was far enough along and had enough bipartisan support that there was a rally opportunity to bring the bill to the floor during this unorthodox December session. The TVPRA passed on December 10, 2008.

Sitting in the Roosevelt Room, celebrating the efforts of so many, I hoped that these new policies would truly be the first step to ending modern-day slavery in this country and around the world. At that moment I felt gratitude, above all things. I was grateful that Tom was willing to take a risk on a young leader just starting my career, grateful for the support

I sought and received from people who had decades more policy and political expertise, and grateful that I had a cause to fight for that was so much bigger than my own fears or insecurities.

TAKEAWAYS

Our work on the reauthorization of the TVPA was a clear case of betting on the little guy—we had to bring all of the different coalition members together to address a big issue, despite their different opinions and skills. It is a good example of understanding unique windows of opportunity that may open without planning and can close without notice if you're not paying attention and nimble enough to act. It is also the story of an incredible visionary and philanthropist who put her heart and her wallet in the right place at the right time. Philanthropists can frequently be adversaries to advocacy, as they often believe and are advised that advocacy can't be funded. Pam knew advocacy was critical, and she proved that private money well spent can make a huge difference when a partnership with government is formed. If you ever find yourself in a similar situation, here are some of my recommendations.

First, be willing to capitalize on serendipitous moments.

This whole idea would not have come together had Pam asked me about trafficking legislation a few years earlier. The whole movement clicked because of the combination of Pam's questions and the movie company's desire for publicity. Had either of those come at a different time, the idea would not have succeeded. Moments like these are rare, but when you stumble upon one, you need to make the most of it. I had met Pam through a mutual friend years ago, and all of this started from a casual chat we had at a completely unrelated meeting. Sometimes your network will provide you with exactly the coincidence you need to get something started. Don't throw that away.

Second, don't be afraid of strange bedfellows.

Many of the groups in our coalition had fundamentally different opinions, especially on issues related to sex trafficking. As we began to form the coalition, this often caused conflict, but we were able to get everyone to work together. It can be a challenge to ask people to put aside their ideological differences, but in this case the overall issue was so important that it was evident everyone needed to work together to create the amendments and get the bill passed. Because we had put in the hard work of making a bipartisan strategy in forming the coalition, we were able to effectively move our bill through Congress.

Third, never underestimate the importance of macro-level thinking.

When we started working with the coalition members, they were all operating at a very micro level, working with a specific population on a specific aspect of trafficking. While that kind of work is important, getting bills passed is a much broader effort. You need to be able to see the big picture and connect all of the smaller aspects together. In order to have a successful coalition, we had to teach the coalition members to see the bigger picture and to really think about what could be done to improve the TVPA. Ultimately, our resolutions were successful because they addressed these greater issues.

KEY QUOTES AND LESSONS

- A single-funder coalition is subject to the whims of the funder—which in this case was an asset. But philanthropists usually have staff or advisors whose interests may not align with yours. Beware in such cases.
- You need a hook, line, and sinker to get a project started. It is ineffective to move forward with campaigns that simply state problems—you're only achieving one-third of your goal. The problem needs to have credible evidence and a solution proposed. That's the trifecta.
- Small movements can blossom if you have the right combination of talent and perseverance.

THE THREE P'S FOR HUMAN TRAFFICKING

Policy: Working with the top nonprofit program providers, we confronted the challenges of serving victims of trafficking and slavery with effective and smart policy solutions. Once we had the ask, we were able to easily and simply engage the use of *Amazing Grace* and moviegoers into the campaign. We could not have done that effectively unless we did the policy work.

Politics: The ability to effectively use the movie to muster constituents around the country gave us a pop. Most members of Congress were unaware of the issue, so it seemed to come out of nowhere to them, but they couldn't ignore the messages. I would also say it helped that this issue had service providers that were rooted in the faith community. They helped us keep the issue alive after the movie, and they appealed to faith-based Republicans for support. Progressive Democrats didn't need a whole lot of convincing once we made the problem clear and current, but adding Republicans (and especially the conservative Christians) got us a bipartisan appeal that was a winner.

Press: The movie had a bunch of PR money and attention as it came out, and we rode that wave effectively. However, once the movie left theaters, we needed to sustain the validation of public attention, and we did that using celebrities like Ricky Martin and Daryl Hannah. But I think one of the more effective press actions we took was to use the organizations, their memberships, and their stories to try to gain attention. In this coalition we had the church community engaged—churches can be great pathways to public validation and attention. When pastors wrote op-eds or letters to the editors, whole communities (elected officials included) paid just a little bit more attention. A good press strategy looks at the small hits, like a local letter to the editor, and large hits, like a *New York Times* feature, with equal strategic measures. We played the whole field and did so successfully.

CHAPTER 5

One Voice Against Cancer

"Create and foster a spirit of coopetition"

SOMEWHERE IN THE ARCHIVES of the Sheridan Group there is a picture of about sixty advocates poised on the steps of the Capitol, all wearing yellow One Voice Against Cancer T-shirts over their suits and dresses. It was our first lobby day as an organization, and everyone was excited and ready to go. The months leading up to that day had been very tough, full of infighting, deep tensions, and competition, but everyone had shown up regardless. About a week after that event a friend who worked on Capitol Hill asked me, "Are you behind all those cancer people in yellow T-shirts? They were everywhere. I've never seen the cancer groups do anything together before!" I can remember thinking that we had achieved exactly what I had hoped for: the cancer groups were finally united.

Cancer is the second leading cause of death in the United

States and is responsible for almost one out of every four deaths, according to the Centers for Disease Control and Prevention. The American Cancer Society estimates that approximately 40 percent of men and women will be diagnosed with cancer at some point in their lifetime, and the medical costs for cancer in the United States are staggering. Anyone who has heard a doctor say the word *cancer* knows the chill and fear that comes from those words. I have heard those words myself a number of times in my life, from my doctor as well as doctors of the people I love the most. My beloved grandmother died of ovarian cancer nine harrowing months after diagnosis. In 2010, my mother heard "It's cancer" from her own doctor. She was diagnosed with stage 3 lung cancer, despite being a nonsmoker—the cancer cells were already in her lymph nodes and spreading through her body. She had always said that she didn't want to go through chemo like her mother did, but my siblings and dad implored her to think about it and try the new advances in treatment.

On the afternoon before my mom was scheduled for surgery, I was scheduled to give the pep talk at the annual advocacy day we put on for the One Voice Against Cancer coalition. The advocacy day consists of about 250 people hitting the Hill together to support federal cancer funding. I normally give a speech to up the energy and impart confidence. I'd planned to give my traditional rah-rah lines, but spontaneously I went off script. I told the audience to hit the Hill with passion, to make sure everyone they spoke to knew that real lives hang in the balance. "These aren't budget numbers; they represent my mother's chances of survival," I told them. Then I found myself talking about my own cancer scare, when a colonoscopy revealed a mass that required surgery. I didn't realize until that second that I'd never told anyone outside a small circle of family and friends about that experience, which ended with the finding of a benign growth after a week of tense waiting for pathology results.

So many young people, especially men, aren't so lucky. Just six months after my scare, a dear friend, former employee, and young father was diagnosed at thirty-six. He had ignored symptoms for six months, and he died less than a year after his surgery, leaving his young wife and one-year-old son behind. To this day it was the saddest funeral I ever attended. It shook me to my core. In telling these stories, after just three minutes I had personalized cancer in front of 250 people who only knew me as their strategist. When training and speaking I always tell audiences that powerful advocacy starts with passion, frequently passion rooted in a deep personal space. On this particular day and in front of this audience, I took my personal passion directly into the advocacy we all were about to share. It wasn't theoretical for me or for any of those participating. Politics is personal, and it takes a bit of courage to out yourself sometimes, but it is necessary if you want to connect in the moment. To this day people come up to me and tell me it was the most powerful moment of their advocacy experience with OVAC.

In the end my mom reluctantly agreed to chemo—six treatments. She made it through three, and then she could not endure it anymore. We pushed back: "Mom, you raised us all to be fighters, not quitters. We don't give up." She simply said she had decided. Her doctors backed her up and told us that if she didn't have the strength to do it, we should listen to her. We did. After that she went for checks every six months, and for four and a half years she got clean scans—only one more to go and she would officially be in remission. Just one month shy of that last scan my Mom felt crushing pain in her hip the day after Thanksgiving. A week later she got the final diagnosis. The cancer was back: in her bones, lung, and liver. She had months to live. She died on July 4, 2016, a month shy of her seventy-ninth birthday. There are no members of my family who aren't cancer advocates now. Once you lose someone you love to this disease, you quickly realize that we must all try our best to stop it or at least greatly improve how we manage cancer treatments.

Given the alarming statistics and the number of personal tragedies, you would think that the cancer community would be well represented in Washington, focused on getting the funds to continue the search for a cure. However, before 2000 this could not have been further from the truth. The American Cancer Society (ACS) was founded in 1913 and had been educating the public and advocating in Washington for years, but they were not popular with the newer "body part" groups, which focused on specific types of cancer. These newer groups were bold, brazen, dynamic, and nimble. They were fueled by a passion that was not hobbled by bureaucracy and took a new approach that brought attention and rapid success. I knew many of the leaders of these groups because the AIDS movement had inspired them. Many of them had come to me for advice on how to build successful movements around specific diseases, and they had been remarkably successful in achieving their goals. The ACS had underestimated the power of the groups until it was too late to contain their breakaway efforts, and the cancer community was incredibly fragmented.

At the time there were more than forty different cancer advocacy organizations constantly competing with each other for funding. The ACS was the behemoth in the group and viewed the other groups as competitors, threats, and annoyances. They had no desire to facilitate strategies or policy initiatives that were responsive to the body part organizations, and the body part groups were often too busy warring between themselves to even care. There was no cohesion, no unity, no common goals.

I can remember working with the AIDS lobby and telling people that we were successful precisely because we weren't the cancer community. We would have a letter signed by over a hundred organizations agreeing on the amount of money the AIDS community wanted from national public health agencies, and the cancer community would be literally fighting with each other in the hallways of Congress, unable to make any progress. Everyone agreed that fighting cancer should be a top funding priority, but no one could agree on how that funding should be distributed. If one group got more than the others, they would turn on one another instantly.

Politicians didn't want to get in the middle of a fight between cancer groups, so they would just walk away. As a result their funding suffered. It was truly a shark tank: highly competitive, personally venomous, notoriously backbiting, and decidedly ineffective. Groups fought sometimes over merit but more often on turf or bragging rights: an incredible waste of time and effort. I had always stayed on the sidelines, keeping my ideas to myself, but in spring of 1999 I found myself with the opportunity to try to turn the cancer community around.

The CEO of the ACS at that time was John Seffrin. He had been the CEO since 1992 and had been a volunteer there for many years. I had gotten to know John through the antitobacco coalition and we had a strong respect for one another, so when he asked me for my opinion on the overall effectiveness of the cancer community and my views on the ACS's lobbying team, I told him the truth. As I saw it, he desperately needed a change of leadership in his Washington office. It would take a change at the top to make any progress. John asked me for recommendations of people who could fill the position, and while I didn't have any good suggestions at the time, a serendipitous lunch meeting a few weeks later would prove to be the start of a huge change in the cancer community.

My friend Dan Smith had been chief of staff for Senator Tom Harkin of Iowa for four years, and when we met for lunch he told me he was thinking about leaving Capitol Hill and looking for a new job. I knew Dan would be great for the ACS, and I immediately recommended him to John. Dan was quickly hired to become head of government relations for the ACS, and he and I had an honest conversation about the state of the cancer lobby. I wanted to make sure he knew the mess he was about to get into. I also had a plan for how to fix things. For years I had had an idea of how to help the cancer groups, but there hadn't been a leader I could give the idea to, and I didn't want to get involved without having a leadership organization as my client. I've always liked challenges. Here I saw an opportunity to prove that this dysfunctional group could be organized and start to function effectively. The ACS had the resources to make a difference and they also had a serious problem within the community that they needed to solve. Dan has been with me on this work since the start and provides a second view at the end of this chapter.

My idea was for a coalition paid for by the ACS, run by the Sheridan Group, and open to all cancer groups. The coalition would focus exclusively on budget and appropriations, with the goal of getting enough funding that it could be split between the groups when it came down to the specifics. The Sheridan Group was nearly ten years old at that point and had a reputation for being the leading strategist and facilitator of coalitions in DC, particularly for the nonprofit community. We were known for our capacity to put people together who were hard to work with and then creating a successful outcome. This opportunity was perfect for us, and I was confident we were the right people for the job.

Dan loved the idea and introduced me to one of my favorite terms: *coopetition*. In this case, groups would be cooperative on the big numbers and competitive on the smaller line items. It would take many more meetings to hammer out the details of the new coalition, but we always stuck true to that original plan. In addition to embracing coopetition we also developed a "bake a bigger pie; slices are up for grabs" model. If a group wanted to join the coalition they had to be willing to work with the other groups in order to increase overall cancer funding, and then they could compete to get their specific slice of the pie. The converse was also true: if you didn't work well with others and do your part, you'd be disadvantaged when it came time to share in the benefits. When working in politics, a basic Darwinian factor dominates the process. It's essential for effective change makers to always be aware of this dynamic and to toughen up to it as soon as possible.

———

In January 2000 One Voice Against Cancer (OVAC) was founded, with the goal of substantially increasing federal funding to help cancer patients and their families. We hoped that an increase in federal funding would allow for more cutting-edge research, a better quality and availability of care, and an enhanced capacity for prevention, screening, and detection. In addition to our major funding goals, we also had objectives, including creating a benevolent leadership role for the ACS, eliminating the negative competition between cancer groups, and creating a new political force for cancer. We didn't just want to increase funds; we wanted to change the way cancer groups operated.

That first year of OVAC was truly a challenge. The ACS paid us to facilitate the development and strategy of the coalition. This allowed Dan to chair the effort but left the strategy and direction up to us. Because he was new to the cancer community Dan acted as a humble leader, almost more like a peer, which diffused some of the negativity around ACS, enabling them to work more cooperatively with others. We had to set up a model for the coalition itself, figure out the strengths of the organizations we were working with, create targets, and then focus on the policies we would be working to change. Our goals were ambitious, and we knew the stakes were high. The United States needed to put more funding toward fighting cancer, and this was our one chance to turn a dysfunctional community into an efficient lobbying force.

From the start it was rough going. All of the smaller cancer groups hated the ACS just as much as they hated each other, so it took some big steps from the ACS to prove that they were willing to cooperate. The ACS had to back away from pushing their own interests in order to show the others that they valued the collective. The success of the ACS's efforts was mostly accomplished by Dan's leadership style: he was laid-back, calm, and generous and deferred to colleagues at every opportunity. It was obvious that the ACS was paying for all of OVAC's efforts, from the catering at meetings to the sponsorship of the annual lobby day, but Dan never used that to his advantage. He curated an air of benevolence and humility that was essential to the success of OVAC.

OVAC could not have held together at the beginning without a neutral party present at the negotiations, and that's where the Sheridan Group stepped in. The cancer community had been so contentious for so long that it was hard for people to put aside their grudges. I described myself as the ombudsman; anyone with a trust issue or a perceived conflict with another coalition member was welcome to come to my office for a discussion and a pledge to try to resolve it. I was fair, but tough; when discipline needed to be enforced, it was my job, and when commitments weren't met, it was my job to call and make sure things kept moving. I had served in this sort of role at the inception of the AIDS lobby, and the reputation for doing it well had stuck. I was there to manage the process to make sure that we achieved our goals, enabling us to reward groups for their cooperation. I had a relationship with most of the groups, so they knew I was serious and not very tolerant of drama and internal nonsense. Frankly, it was sometimes tiring to always be the bad cop, and I will admit I sometimes lost patience with all the infighting. But in the end I knew it was a necessary role for someone to play; without an ombudsman at the table there would be no common ground and the entire effort would fail.

Early on the decision had been made to focus exclusively on budget and appropriations, which was the best way to get a big pie that could then be divvied up among our various groups. Each line item in the budget had to be debated, and we spent endless hours in meetings trying to hammer out compromises. One of our ground rules for OVAC priorities was that a member organization had to take the responsibility to do the work to prepare a budget request and do credible work creating a justification for it. Each year we'd gather for a full day and debate the merits of each organization's request. If no one showed up to propose the line item, we did not include it. If an organization only showed up at the annual meeting but didn't do any work the rest of the year, their request had to come with an explicit commitment for improved participation, done publicly in front of the entire group. No free rides were allowed.

That yearly meeting was always a struggle to find the right combination of increases in spending and strong justifications. Not all organizations had the same level of policy expertise; most didn't have keen political instincts. They varied widely between hopeless optimists and constrained conservatives. The breakdown of how individual cancer groups usually requested funds occurred along common fault lines—the smaller cancer groups that perceived themselves to be ignored or unfairly treated in budget allocations went high—payback for past slights. In those days the very aggressive and successful National Breast Cancer Coalition was the enemy—their success was perceived as a loss for prostate cancer or lung cancer. Other cancers affecting women, such as ovarian cancer, raged over the lack of balance in funding cancers affecting women generally. In those early meetings it felt like refereeing a Hobson's choice convention. Leveling the playing field so everyone felt heard and respected and ensuring that the funding requests were politically relevant took hours of debate and weeks of back-channel negotiations and coaching. I remember spending a few days a week for well over a month just helping the lung cancer coalition understand the NIH funding process and why their requests needed to meet a justification standard that was greater than "we want that number because it is what breast cancer gets and we have more patients than they do." Reaching consensus was never easy, but once we reached an agreement—and we always did—each organization had to be committed to carrying the whole plan. No side deals were allowed, all materials had to carry the overall ask, and each organization's individual lobby materials had to endorse the OVAC numbers.

Dan's relationship with Senator Harkin was incredibly helpful in getting everyone on board, as during those years Harkin was either the chairman or the ranking member of the appropriations committee that decided on the funding for the NIH and the CDC, the two largest budgets of the public health effort on cancer. Everyone in the coalition was well aware of the consequences of offending or crossing Dan and how that could easily be passed on to Senator Harkin. And while Dan was careful never to threaten or intimidate, I could occasionally hint at this connection and use it as a bargaining chip for better cooperation from coalition members. Very early on in the OVAC development process, one particular cancer group made a rather bold move to undermine Dan's leadership and split the coalition into factions. Their strategy was divisive: they said you could either be part of their group (focused mostly on research and pharmaceuticals) or be part of OVAC. It was ridiculously immature, a high school lunch room move. Dan simply told the new OVAC membership that there were no choices necessary— everyone was welcome at the OVAC table regardless of affiliations with other firms, coalitions, or groups. As Michelle Obama famously stated, "When they go low, we go high."

One particularly successful funding effort came from Paula Kim, the co-founder of the Pancreatic Cancer Action Network. She wanted to prioritize the deadliest cancers and pointed out to me that while funding had grown for the larger cancer demographics like breast cancer and lung cancer, the cancers that were the deadliest, like pancreatic cancer and brain cancer, were far behind in funding for both prevention and care. She and I worked together to get the OVAC community to embrace a "seven deadly cancers" initiative that raised those budgets proportionally higher each year for five years. The key to this was to assure all the coalition members that this initiative was a rising tide; its success would not come at the price of other success, but would instead create political capital to keep all the line items growing.

Other groups were less successful because they were unable to use this sort of approach. There are multiple programs and line items in the federal budget that help support cancer research, treatment, and care, either directly or indirectly. We were able to carefully choose the line items that we viewed as in need of additional money and/or policy language, and then focus all of our attention on those items. When our rogue colleagues simply didn't do well (or as well) in the budget and appropriations bills, we were clear with our coalition members why that was the case. There must be consequences for actions that are undermining the goals of an entire community, and the only consequence that matters in the advocacy game is a loss. Political actions and behaviors have to be appropriately rewarded or punished. The National Breast Cancer Coalition (NBCC) never joined OVAC, and while other breast cancer groups were able to keep OVAC focused on their funding goals, the NBCC's attempts to get more funding from the Department of Defense were ultimately unsuccessful. Yes, OVAC supported the NIH and CDC line items for breast cancer, but we didn't carry the DOD line item that NBCC had exclusively valued. In moments like this it is important to keep your mind on the real goals; we could only be successful if we stayed focused on getting better cancer treatments and working toward a cure.

Billions of dollars were at stake, and we were always careful to ensure that the tenor of our work and our rules reflected that. If a group went off and presented their own numbers to members of Congress, they were treated harshly by the rest of the group: board members were called and policy staff on Capitol Hill were told to no longer trust that group. After we won a CDC line item for the International Melanoma Foundation, they stopped participating and left the group. They were never welcomed back to OVAC, and they never saw another increase to that line item after they won the first round and left. Thankfully, that sort of behavior was a rarity, and for the most part everyone was careful to observe our rules. Competition was only tolerated on the smaller issues within the group; to the members of Congress we worked with we presented a totally unified front. It was important that we were always on message, always presenting the same funding requests.

Our coopetition and slices of the pie approaches proved to be hugely successful. We were first out of the box every year on budget requests across all disease-specific groups and were able to get big numbers on our important goals as well as getting specialty initiatives and programs for the smaller cancer groups. As the biggest player in the game, the ACS was still getting the largest share of the funding, but they were no longer fighting with the smaller groups; their reputation had been restored and their leadership was gaining trust. We had even found a way to incorporate the volunteers from all of the different cancer groups that made up the coalition.

Early on in the creation of OVAC we were trying to figure out how to harness the vast network of volunteers that the different cancer groups relied on. We eventually developed a two-part strategy, focusing both on lobbying in the Capitol and training volunteers in coalition members' home areas. Four times a year a professional team of grassroots trainers would travel the country to put on seminars, seeking to teach cancer advocacy groups how to do effective lobbying, using OVAC as the model. This simple but brilliant idea began to create an arm of well-trained volunteers who made OVAC's budget goals a priority to constituents. Other groups utilized fake grassroots efforts—sometimes called astroturfing, which involved having constituents fax or mail in preprinted messages to Congress. This can be effective for a final push, but we were looking for quality not quantity in our advocates, and so we would train any cancer group that was willing to have us. We wanted real people, real stories, and live phone calls to really make the impression we wanted. These advocacy techniques helped promote the ideas of cooperation and communication that we were trying to establish in every OVAC meeting.

In addition to our work across the country, we instituted an annual lobby day, which has become a huge and successful event for OVAC. We would invite people from across the country to come to Washington, DC, train them on the specific funding asks the coalition had agreed on, and then send them off to Capitol Hill to meet with members of Congress and their staff. I don't remember whose idea it was to make everyone wear yellow OVAC shirts that first year, but those shirts helped to remind everyone that we were now one unified group. A few years later, when the Congressional Management Foundation—a research organization that looks at how Congress functions and what affects it—rated the most effective lobby efforts, the cancer lobby was the only nonprofit public interest issue on their top twenty list. OVAC had made its mark, and its effectiveness was independently validated. That was a particularly proud moment for me. It was now time to join forces with another coalition that had been working hard to increase the budget of the NIH.

In the late 1990s, Congress had made a commitment to double the NIH's budget by 2003. In the forty years before that, the NIH's budget had doubled on average every ten years, so this commitment sped up the usual process and was obviously going to require a lot of cooperation. A group had been founded to take on the lobbying work to support the doubling goal, called the Campaign for Medical Research (CMR). CMR was run by Kevin Mathis, with Robert Michel and Paul Rogers as the Republican and Democratic lobbyists, respectively. Most of the work came from the coalition members, operating under a plan similar to OVAC's. I had been keeping an eye on their progress as we developed OVAC. They were really taking on a huge challenge—just to get the cancer groups to identify, prioritize, and agree on the cancer budget was a tall order. To get all the stakeholders around all the money at NIH to agree felt even to me too big to manage. But brilliantly they went for a simple message and simple goal—double the NIH budget in five years. This simplicity stopped what frequently is the breaking point of issue-based efforts—that they get stuck in the weeds, going for perfect when possible would succeed. Once they avoided that trap, we jumped in willingly and enthusiastically. By 2001 I had seen their successes and knew it was time to join forces and really push for those final few years of funding increases.

Much like in the early days of OVAC, the NIH funding effort required many different groups to work together for a common goal. The decision to start working with CMR was not an easy one; OVAC had just started to hit its stride as a cohesive group, and we knew the reason for our success was our focus. If we broadened our agenda to include NIH funding, it could seriously threaten what we had collectively built, and people worried that working with CMR would dilute OVAC's effectiveness. Yet I was firm in my resolution to replicate the successes of the coalition I had formed during my time with the AIDS lobby. A doubling of the NIH budget overall would be a big win for cancer, but a failure to increase the budget would result in a disease war, with everyone scrambling for a piece of the smaller pie. That seemed like an incredible waste of time and resources, and so we joined the fight.

By this time we were big and known for being effective, so lending CMR our support really made a difference. Part of what made our partnership so strong was that, much like Dan's close relationship with Senator Harkin, Kevin had a relationship with Senator Arlen Specter, who was also often the chair of the appropriations committee that funded the NIH. (The majority party of each chamber selects the chairman and leadership of the committees. Tradition has dictated that those assignments are done by seniority, determined by years served. Recently the Republicans have term-limited their leaders, allowing only six consecutive years as a chairman of a committee or subcommittee. Each party in each chamber has its own rules, but the majority party always gets the chair, with the minority party designated as ranking member.) In this situation, we had the perfect inside/outside collaboration between OVAC, CMR, and the two senators. In the end, our efforts were successful: the NIH's budget was successfully doubled, and a large portion of the extra funding was directed toward cancer research.

The cancer community had come a long way from those fractious days in the nineties. Turning around such a dysfunctional group had required a lot of hard work, but we ended up with a coalition we could be proud of and some very clear successes. Our efforts were clearly evident in the rapid advance of medical research in the years following the increase in the NIH budget. Smaller cancer groups that worked hard were rewarded with specialty initiatives or programs that were unique to their needs. OVAC always focused on winning the big-picture goals but consistently made sure some of the "small stuff" got attention, too.

For the ACS in particular, this effort was a triple bottom-line winner: they got big numbers on important goals, including a 400 percent increase in cancer research funding at the NIH and CDC; they got the lion's share of funding as the biggest player; and they restored their reputation and solidified relationships that they badly needed if they wanted to maintain leadership. As I write these words I'm struck by how far cancer research and treatment have come. The progress of research that was catalyzed by this important coalition effort has changed the cancer landscape in profound ways: Gleevec was discovered for the treatment of leukemia; the advent of proteomics to pinpoint proteins in cancer cells and design treatments has led to breakthroughs in lung cancer treatment; the gene mapping that leads cancer prevention and early detection has created a pathway to prevention protocols we could not have imagined when OVAC began. The Sheridan Group's work on this campaign remains an example of a relatively simple, inexpensive effort that truly changed the world. As with so many of the issues and campaigns we've worked on, this battle is not over. Cancer has not been cured, but the last twenty years have led to transformative progress, and in that we see hope.

Second View: Dan Smith

After spending a decade of my career on the Hill working in a variety of capacities for Senator Tom Harkin, including four years as chief of staff and two and a half years as staff director of the Agriculture Committee, I was hired to be the new vice president for government relations for the American Cancer Society in 1999. I came into that job knowing a lot about Congress and how decisions were made and virtually nothing about the cancer community in Washington, DC.

During the time I worked for Senator Harkin he served as both chairman and ranking member of the Labor, Health and Human Services, and Education Appropriations Subcommittee, and while I was not running that subcommittee day to day, I sat in on

Dancing with "Nana Biggins" (aka Mary Ellen Biggins née Murphy). *(Courtesy of the author)*

The Sheridan Family at my mother's 70th birthday party in Lewes, Delaware. *(Courtesy of the author)*

Our wedding photo at Lewes, with Phina *(right)*, the flower girl, and Duffy *(left)*, the ring-bearer. *(Courtesy of Denis Reggie)*

A feature article in *The Hill* newspaper (June 10, 2008). *(Courtesy of The Hill)*

The actual roll call in the Senate on passage of the Ryan White CARE Act, signed and given to me by Senator Kennedy. The inscription reads: "To Tom: What happened to those other 4?" (referring to the four senators who voted NO). *(Courtesy of the author)*

Jeanne White at the signing ceremony for "The Reauthorization of the Ryan White CARE Act." George H. W. Bush had refused to grant us a signing ceremony for the original, but Bill Clinton granted the request the second time around. *(Courtesy of CHUCK KENNEDY/AFP/Getty Images)*

Jeanne White and me at the AmFAR dinner in New York in 1991. *(Courtesy of the author)*

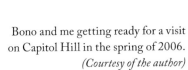

Bono and me getting ready for a visit on Capitol Hill in the spring of 2006. *(Courtesy of the author)*

President Bush signing PEPFAR. Behind him is Senator John Kerry *(beige suit)*, who wrote the original draft of the bill. *(Courtesy of JIM WATSON/AFP/Getty Images)*

Civil disobedience demonstration on the Capitol Steps to raise awareness for the Americans with Disabilities Act. *(Courtesy of Tom Olin/Disability History Museum)*

Human trafficking and slavery affect people all over the world and is most pernicious in forced-labor factories, like this brick making company in Africa. *(Courtesy of Humanity United by Daniel Lin)*

The first Capitol Hill event for OVAC: A milestone of cooperation in an otherwise contentious community. *(Courtesy of American Cancer Society Cancer Action Network, Inc.)*

With Hillary Clinton in Manchester, New Hampshire, prior to taping a "Conversation with the Candidates" segment sponsored by Save the Children Action Network. Sponsoring this series was the best strategic move for SCAN in 2016; every Democratic candidate and all but two of the Republicans participated. *(Courtesy of the author)*

Mark Shriver, CEO of Save the Children Action Network, at an early childhood education center in West Virginia. *(Courtesy of Eli Murray/ Save the Children)*

Onstage presenting the "America Forward" concept to "The Gathering of Leaders" at Mohonk Mountain House in February 2007: *(left to right)* Scott Hatch (my Republican counterpart), Shirley Sagawa (co-author of our America Forward book), and me. *(Courtesy of New Profit)*

With Walter Mondale at his campaign staff reunion in 2016. This is the only photo I ever took with him deliberately. *(Courtesy of the author)*

The Sheridan Group staff retreat in Lewes, Delaware, in 2016. Senator Harris Wofford *(front right)* died on January 21, 2019 (RIP). *(Courtesy of the author)*

Victoria Reggie Kennedy and Phyllis Segal at the anniversary celebration for AmeriCorps on the White House lawn. *(Courtesy of the author)*

Vince and me with Senator Chris Coons, a champion and friend, in Lewes. *(Courtesy of the author)*

AmeriCorps Cape Cod member Brad Falco performing a prescribed burn for wildfire fuel reduction and habitat restoration in Wellfleet, Massachusetts. *(Courtesy of Ameri-Corps Cape Cod)*

AnnMaura Connelly, chair of Voices for National Service, presenting our annual champion award to Senator Chris Coons (D-DE). *(Courtesy of Elliot Haney for City Year)*

many meetings where important decisions were made regarding funding levels. One thing I knew for sure (having been in "the room where it happens") was that when communities sought funding for their important projects, especially disease groups, it was important to present a united front and make their best case to the appropriators. Communities fighting among themselves greatly harm their cause, because no politician wants to step into a nasty internal community battle. This basic knowledge helped me understand that the cancer community could do better by working more closely together (rather than body part by body part), and so I went to work with my good friend Tom Sheridan to form a new coalition of cancer groups to work together to increase funding for important cancer research and prevention programs at the NIH and CDC.

There were many challenges as Tom and I worked together to form this new coalition. Many in the cancer community were suspicious of ACS, wary of what ACS wanted out of this new coalition, and skeptical ACS would share credit. Years of strain and mistrust between ACS and some smaller cancer groups was a preexisting condition we had to tackle. As Tom often said, "I didn't pack those bags, but unfortunately, I have to carry them." Building trust is an essential part of new coalition building, and we worked hard to overcome these issues. I made sure to listen to everyone's ideas, craft a logical agenda that had something for everyone involved, and gave away the credit whenever possible. Tom and his firm served as the neutral ombudsman allowing coalition members to vent frustrations in a safe space, be heard, and have their opinions acted upon. Smaller cancer groups knew that Tom had my ear and we would work hard to address their needs.

Some groups never did come on board, but one of the keys to building a coalition is to not let a couple of naysayers stop you from moving forward—hard as they may try. If you have a good idea and you are willing to stand behind it and take the slings and arrows, that idea will prevail. Seventeen years later, One Voice Against Cancer continues to be strong. I am enormously proud of the work we did to make this happen and result in billions of additional dollars dedicated to cancer research and prevention.

TAKEAWAYS

I have never seen such an unproductive group as the cancer community in the 1990s. Nothing was being achieved, and yet cancer was affecting more and more of the general population. A drastic change was needed in order to achieve success. If you ever find yourself trying to corral such a fractious set of players, there are some important things you should keep in mind.

First, never underestimate the power of a neutral convener on a discordant community.

There was no way for any of the current groups to suddenly break out of the infighting and establish a peaceful coalition. While it was the ACS that technically established OVAC, they were not going to be able to sit at the table with the other groups and enforce order from the start. My presence and that of my staff at those early meetings allowed OVAC to prosper, as we were able to facilitate when conflicts arose and generally keep the different groups aimed toward the same goal. If there is tension and mistrust between the groups, you need to remember that time and shared experiences can heal those wounds. A well-known, well-respected third party can often speed up this process.

Second, humility can breed success, even for big-name groups.

The ACS has been around for many years, but they were getting nowhere due to their fights with the smaller, newer cancer groups. Once we convinced them to establish OVAC and back off a bit from their own self-interests, the smaller groups came to see the ACS as a benevolent leader instead of a divisive enemy. As a result, the ACS got the funding they wanted, and the smaller groups did as well: everyone prospered. This sort of approach is not easy or simple. It requires a commitment from the senior leadership of a big organization to humble themselves in this manner. Dan's leadership skills were essential in bridging the gap between OVAC members and the senior leadership of ACS—he knew it was crucial to make sure the ACS leadership understood and valued their commitment to OVAC.

Third, having a clear, identifiable set of goals is incredibly important.

In the early days of OVAC, we spent a lot of time going over our agenda and choosing the budget items we wanted to fight for. We didn't want to take over the world; we just wanted to solve one big problem. The budget and appropriations process is by no means simple, but it does work in an established time frame with clear, quantifiable results. This made it easier to create a focus, establish goals, and figure out what resources from the different groups we would need in order to succeed. Knowing that our main goal was to increase cancer funding overall, the smaller groups were willing to compete over the smaller issues; if we met our big goals, they knew they would reap the benefits. Having goals was also useful when talking to the people in Congress, as every meeting they had with someone in the cancer community went the same way. There was no confusion over which parts of the budget were important to us; we were able to clearly state our goals in every meeting we had on Capitol Hill. In the end, everyone has to see that they can and will win, or the reason for playing together doesn't make sense.

KEY QUOTES AND LESSONS

- Recognize the value of coopetition.
- Bake a bigger pie; then slices are up for grabs.
- Humble leadership is often required as a first step.
- When swimming in a shark tank, make sure your stroke is strongest.
- Combine your assets, assess their strengths, and deploy them carefully. You don't need quantity as much as quality when building movements.
- Focus will always help you make clear decisions. There will be distractions, but you must dismiss them if you want to succeed.

THE THREE P'S FOR OVAC

Policy: Finding a policy position that allowed competing and antagonistic cancer advocates to coalesce was not easy. There is a fine line between too much detail, where disagreements are always petty and unproductive, and too little detail, where it's not clear what success really looks like in the end. For OVAC we found the "just right" spot by doing two things: being very narrow in our focus on only budget and appropriations for cancer funding, and establishing a clear rule that a coalition member in good standing had to support any request the overall coalition carried. In the end, this allowed us to have clear and measurable goals, allowed each coalition member a priority to justify their engagement and work, and created accountability that was mutual across all coalition members. Our policy was created annually at an all-day meeting in January (before the budget and appropriations processes begin), and each line item was presented by a member organization for review and discussion. It was a long day every year, but once we'd decided on our requests we had our policy ask for the year, and from there on out the work was about achieving goals, not debating process and substance. This all-day meeting proved to be extremely effective.

Politics: The political challenges for OVAC were multifaceted—internally within the individual groups, externally with Congress, and specifically focused on the ACS's role and leadership. It is not an overstatement to say our biggest political challenges were indeed internal to the cancer community itself. The competition, resentments, and distrust within the community were singularly blocking any path to effective external politics. Resolving that was the most important step. The ACS had the resources, and in Dan it had an opportunity to present a new leadership model, but it was distrusted and disliked by a nearly unanimous "body parts" lobby. The need to coalesce was blocked by a resistance to the ACS's leadership. Our breakthrough was the fact that Dan's relationship with Senator Harkin was an asset none of the groups could afford to squander—it was never said, threatened, or used overtly, but it was understood, and it provided the impetus to create and mature OVAC. Once we got the groups on board, working effectively and trusting each other, the politics of Capitol Hill fell easily and successfully into place.

Press: Our press strategy was simple and straightforward. We didn't need to create a reason to prioritize cancer—every reporter had their own experiences and stories. Our challenge was to make it feel more urgent, make it more politically necessary to take bold actions, and hold politicians more accountable if they failed to act. We also used the creation of the coalition to grab a little attention. The press had covered the now infamous AIDS lobby, and this was a second-generation story—how cancer advocates learned to do it differently and better. AIDS had the press angle of ACT UP—cancer wasn't going to get that kind of activism or drama. On our first OVAC Lobby Day, we dressed 250 advocates in bright yellow T-shirts and posed them on the steps of the Capitol for a photo op. We got a multitude of uses from that photo, and it made an important impression. In addition, we used cancer advocates to write letters to the editor and op-eds for local newspapers, and to attend editorial board meetings. Members of Congress read the local papers more thoroughly than they read the *New York Times* or the *Washington Post*. Cancer patients and families have powerful, heartwarming, and heartrending stories to tell, and we were able to harness those stories and always, always put the ask at the end. It wasn't fancy, but it was effective.

CHAPTER 6

Save the Children
Action Network

"Betray conventional wisdom and think bigger"

SAVE THE CHILDREN USA (STC) was founded in the United States in 1932, with a mission to protect children around the world, aiming to give them "a healthy start, the opportunity to learn, and protection from harm." When Hurricane Katrina swept through in 2005, it became clear that the United States was unprepared to effectively help children right here in our own country after disasters. More than five thousand children were reported missing after the hurricane, and it took six months to find them all. It took a catastrophe like Katrina for people to realize that there were more comprehensive disaster plans for pets than there were for children in the United States, which was obviously unacceptable.

The story of my involvement with Save the Children began shortly after Katrina. In early 2006 I had breakfast with Mark Shriver, vice president for US programs for STC.

Mark and I had been friends for years and worked together informally on a number of things, but now he wanted to call me in. He thought STC would gain value from my input on how to become better prepared nationally for the next big disaster—and more than that, how to wake people up to the disaster in our midst that STC was working to solve every day. Mark invited me to be a part of their brainstorming and the transformational work that followed, including the Congressionally mandated National Commission on Children and Disasters.

Success on one issue can frequently be an invitation to do more work together in the future, and nearly a decade later Mark and I were once again having breakfast when he expressed his total frustration about recent funding efforts for family and kids in poverty in the US. His job as senior vice president for domestic programs at Save the Children required that he travel to nearly every state legislature in the country, hat in hand, asking for funding, and what he usually got was a pat on the head. Or he would get showered with praise, told he was doing God's work, and then, in a backroom deal somewhere, the funding for programs for the neediest children in the state was eliminated from the budget. He was at the end of his rope and had started thinking that maybe he didn't want to be involved in this kind of work anymore. As he told me this, I asked what he thought about changing the situation entirely. I had experienced some of the same kinds of frustration while working at the Child Welfare League, and so I had actually spent time thinking about how things could be better. I told him that perhaps if he could create something that could actually put accountability into politics, he would have a lot less of that sort of treatment and would instead get more respect. That conversation was the spark of what would eventually become Save the Children Action Network (SCAN), a powerful new 501(c)(4).

From the beginning, Mark and I were a very good team. I developed the ideas, framework, and strategy, and Mark provided substance and a solid political network we could use. The end result was the National Commission on Children and Disasters. It took a few months to get the legislation drafted and passed and three long years to get it up and running and completed. But it was well worth it. Between the commission and STC's new focus on domestic disaster preparedness, people in the United States were better prepared to protect children in the event of a disaster.

I was proud of what we had accomplished, but my work with Mark was far from over. We had become close during the long years of working on the commission, and it was around this time that we had that brainstorming breakfast meeting and came up with the plan for a new organization that could lobby for children. STC was a 501(c)(3) and was thus prohibited from engaging in political campaigns. A 501(c)(4), however, was free to lobby aggressively and participate in political elections, promoting issues and holding elected officials accountable at the ballot box. I felt that if we could convince STC to create a 501(c)(4), we could make some real progress on the issues that were important to Mark and the other people at STC.

Mark and I both knew this was going to be a tough sell.

STC had never done anything like this before. Presenting our idea turned out to be a multistep process that happened over the course of nearly a year. The first thing we did was to meet with Carolyn Miles, the new president and CEO of STC. She had been in the job for only a short while, but to her credit she immediately saw the benefits of our proposition. She asked Mark to look into the feasibility of creating a 501(c)(4), which we then brought back to show the board. The board then asked for a detailed business plan for the new organization, complete with governance, goals, fund-raising, staffing, risk mitigation for the 501(c)(3), and assurances of nonpartisan design.

Understandably, the board was apprehensive about delving into politics, but Mark and I had a strong rationale for this move, and we came prepared with a plan. We made the case that a 501(c)(4) can act as a force multiplier for an organization interested in aggressively pursuing its mission. STC's mission was to solve problems, create solutions, and effect change, all of which was dependent on the role of government and the use of political power. Many in the nonprofit sector ignore that simple fact, but this was our opportunity to change that perspective. So often you see big organizations that have 501(c)(4)s that function as red-headed stepchildren, as it were, created by accountants or lawyers to shield an organization from politics. We wanted to do the opposite, to use our 501(c)(4) to actively engage in politics. When approaching a reluctant board, you have two choices: walk them slowly into a position that can emerge over time, or go bold with a confidence that inspires them to take the risk. We chose the latter. Mark said his vision was to "create the NRA for kids." Mark presents the second view in this chapter, and he unpacks this statement a little more, but basically, he was emphasizing the need to have political clout to get things done. To be successful to funders we needed to be able to insist that people voted how we wanted them to, and we needed to be able to defeat those who defied us. Sadly, the NRA is incredibly effective politically, and we wanted STC to have the same power and capacity but on behalf of America's kids, who don't vote, can't donate, and frequently get left behind on the priorities list.

Throughout this process I became infamous for telling audiences of board members, staff, and donors that political relevance came down to a simple question: "Do you have the capacity to thank and spank?" In other words, can you reward the good and punish the bad? If yes, you can be relevant, and if no, you won't ever really get there. The question has always raised eyebrows, but it does sum up the rawness of politics and its effect on who the winners and losers are in these great debates. Sadly, 99 percent of nonprofits in America fail the "thank/spank" test. While corporate America now has virtually unfettered opportunity to affect politics with money—thanks to the Supreme Court decision in *Citizens United*—nonprofits are legally hamstrung from actions and activities that are core to their missions and services. No wonder you watch Congress ignore the good and reward the bad year after year without consequences. While I abhor the work and tactics of the Koch brothers, you cannot ignore the fact that they are effective. They thank those who serve their interests (Paul Ryan) and spank those who attempt to stop them (Tammy Baldwin). I believe the American public is slowly but deliberately waking up to the corrosive effect of money in politics. That process is slow, and the disinclination of many Americans to do their own homework and fact-checking as opposed to believing the lies of slick commercials and paid social media campaigns is still a very big threat.

SCAN is pioneering in this space. Mark's vision and leadership is audacious. The success of this very aggressive, politically forward-leaning effort will change the paradigm for their priorities and mission, but maybe more important, it will be a case study by which other nonprofits can begin to make big internal changes in order to make the needed changes in the world. This lesson is an important one—organizations, change makers, and leaders cannot create transformative change unless we're ready to make some changes within ourselves and our organizations. Wishing for change, calling for action, and hoping for a better day is frankly meaningless—you have to have capacity and you must push yourself into the uncomfortable places that make you politically relevant.

One of the most controversial aspects of our business plan was our requirement that the board pick two priorities from STC's long list of issues. The new 501(c)(4) would need to focus on just two issues in order to be successful: one domestic and one global. This was difficult for the board and senior staff, as STC had a culture of caring about a wide variety of issues related to children all over the world. I had four criteria in mind when encouraging them to focus on two specific issues: (1) there was real, viable policy work to be done on the issues; (2) STC had expertise in the area but not necessarily grants or money; (3) successful results would be transformative and directly tied to our goals; and (4) the addition of some political muscle would increase the chances of success and gain political capital for the organization. It took a while, but the board eventually picked their two priorities: domestically, we would focus on early childhood education, and globally, we would focus on maternal and newborn child survival.

———————

While it wasn't easy to get the board to pick just two priorities, their selections highlight two crucial issues facing children around the world today. According to STC, in the United States, 16 million children living in poverty enter school unprepared to succeed. These kids start off behind and in many cases never catch up. Research has shown that four-year-olds from low-income families are eighteen months behind other four-year-olds—an alarming gap at such a young age. STC has long been aware that getting children into early education programs can make a huge difference, so SCAN would focus its domestic efforts on improving access to early childhood education across the country.

Globally, however, the issue is still one of survival first and education second. Since 1990, the mortality rate for children under five has dropped 50 percent, according to the World Health Organization, but it is still unacceptably high. UNICEF reports that every day 16,000 children die from preventable and treatable causes such as pneumonia, dehydration, and diarrhea, and that every year, worldwide, approximately 1 million newborns die, and 3 million children die from malnutrition. These are unnecessary, preventable deaths. The global priority at SCAN would be aimed at preventing as many of these needless deaths as possible. The original goal was to halve mortality by 2020 and eradicate preventable death by 2035—ambitious goals, but hugely important ones.

———

After almost a year's hard effort, in 2013 our new 501(c)(4) was created: the Save the Children Action Network (SCAN). Mark became the president and CEO, and with the continued assistance of myself and others at the Sheridan Group, he immediately began looking for new staff to hire. Our goal was to begin our advocacy efforts with state legislative races in 2013 to test-drive our new ideas, and so we needed staff quickly. Our business plan called for a senior management team of four—each with an expertise that would drive effective advocacy efforts: government affairs (lobbying), political action (campaigns and elections), mobilization (grassroots and grasstops—those who are opinion leaders, make political contributions, or have political connections), and communications (earned, paid, and social).

The plan from the beginning was to make SCAN nonpartisan—not bipartisan, where one political party has the ability to torpedo a whole idea, but totally set apart from the political party lines. We had our goals, we had our agenda, and politicians were either going to be with us or against us. Nonpartisanship has been an important guiding principle of SCAN, and it was a factor we considered as we began to staff the senior management team. We wanted top-level talent, regardless of political party, people who had senior levels of experience and proven track records for effective work. The balance of Republicans and Democrats was essential, but talent was our top priority. This turned out to be quite difficult—jobs for senior-level advocacy talent tend to pay well, and the human resources structure of STC did not allow us to offer the high rate of pay these people deserved. Honestly, sometimes we got the talent just because we were lucky: a campaign had ended and someone needed a job, or a new executive cleaned house at a major issue organization and people became available. What made this project interesting to our hires, I think, was that they were basically going into a start-up. They would have free rein to design and build something unique, right from the start. It didn't hurt that Mark is a very charismatic leader; people are attracted to his passion and vision.

Our first hire was Kimberly Robson, the former field director for People for the American Way and NARAL. Our second hire was a Republican, Paul Ciaramitaro. Paul had previously worked on Mitt Romney's campaign and had been a successful manager for Republican state campaigns and ballot initiatives. He became our political director. For communications we recruited Brendan Daly, who had spent nine years as Nancy Pelosi's communications director. The last hire was a Capitol Hill veteran, John Monsif, a former chief of staff to a member from Maryland. In efforts like this one, talent matters, and talent comes with a résumé of performance. These four people would go on to be instrumental in our efforts to make SCAN a true player in politics.

Once we filled out the rest of the team of senior members and then staff, we were ready for our first real advocacy effort. Our plan was to work in a few state senate races, focused entirely on our early childhood education initiatives. State senates have a lot of control over statewide education policy, so those were the races we wanted to influence. For instance, in Iowa that year the state had a surplus and senate Democrats (minority) wanted to spend it on early education. The Republican majority and governor opposed, and we wanted to take them to account for it. In South Carolina they were considering a social impact bond proposal where private and public dollars could be leveraged for the early childhood education programs in the state. We wanted that bill to pass and wanted to elect state senators in support of it, and we also wanted the South Carolina education superintendent to win because she supported it (as a Republican).

One of the most important decisions at SCAN that year was to tell the new senior management team to experiment widely. Any idea they had that they thought would be successful, Mark and I wanted them to try it. We worked to create a culture where people were rewarded instead of penalized for trying new things. We were working in only a few state senate races that year, so, as the stakes were much lower, we had the freedom to experiment. A crucial part of this experimental stage was the data we were able to gather to determine which of our efforts were successful. Our first polling was a pre- and post-test exercise to see exactly which messages and arguments worked best on which demographics of voters. Using pre- and post-test metrics allows you to poll voters to get a baseline of their opinions, and then you treat two or more groups differently: some get mail, some phone calls, some email blasts, some all of the above. Then you poll again to see which strategy or message or combination of strategies and messages had the best outcome in moving voters into positions and actions we desired. This is time-consuming and expensive, normally not what a novice 501(c)(4) could or would do. We pressed our team to consider these kinds of methods, to test different and innovative messages and tactics, but we warned them that the long-term spending and strategic decisions would be made by the evidence produced. Our first year and those first few races were experiments. We tried different things, measured effectiveness, and then decided to scale up or pull out of different tactical strategies.

After polling, we were able to use the findings to refine our messages to certain population groups. For example, we found that older conservative women were extremely willing to support maternal and newborn survival because of their religious values, but that we had to keep abortion totally out of the picture when targeting them. Additionally, we learned that nearly the entire nation supports early childhood education, but divisions pop up once you start to talk about how to pay for it. All of these findings were instrumental in our efforts to start working in specific races across the country.

One of the first issues we confronted was the typical nonprofit culture's disdain for negative messaging tactics. I was sympathetic toward the board's issue with negative campaigning: during my first attempt to run for Congress in my home state of New York, I can remember my advisors telling me that in order to beat an incumbent you have to tell voters why they should not vote for the familiar face instead of presenting yourself in a positive light. At first, I was totally opposed to the idea and insisted that I wanted to run a clean campaign, using just my merits. It didn't take long for my advisors to show me how naïve I was being. They had clear, harsh data that demonstrated that negative messaging was incredibly successful. The senior advisor to my exploratory committee sent me ten pages of data from the previous three election cycles for congressional seats. Each winning campaign had two notes—the negative message and the cost of media buys to promote it. When you saw a campaign that didn't do it—the results were uniformly losses. "Do you understand the point we were trying to make?" he asked at our next meeting. "Yes," I answered, feeling like a second grader caught not doing his homework. "Okay, now we need to focus on your polling. We won't be looking so much at you; we'll be spending time and money finding out why folks don't like the other guy." I learned my lesson. While I hope someday American politics will not rely so much on negative messaging, it is clear that things won't be changing anytime soon.

Now I needed to educate the board the same way, by proving with data that negative messaging could work. This was a part of what I view as the hallmark of effective advocacy: the ability to "thank and spank." In this work there is rarely a reward for doing the right thing, and there are certainly no effective consequences for doing the wrong thing. We wanted to change that equation by thanking people who were supporting early childhood education through their votes on bills and approval of budgets that prioritized programs and proposals we were supporting, and publicly admonishing those who opposed our ideas. We needed to use both approaches if we were going to be successful in showing people that we weren't your usual nonprofit. We didn't want to always play a negative role, but we needed to show that we could do it, and that we could do it well.

A state senator in Iowa was very anti–early childhood education, and we decided to run an ad against him. Since early childhood education was our domestic priority, it was evident to me that the Iowa race was an important opportunity. We used quotes from the senator but made it into a spoof, with a Dr. Seuss–type theme, complete with green eggs and ham and lines like "Pre-K helps our kids succeed. Chelgren opposed it. Yes indeed." This elected official had actually compared early childhood education to Nazi indoctrination camps for kids. He cast those as pro–early childhood education as "anti-family" and said such programs equaled the "government stealing children." It was so outrageous that we had to confront the messages, but our counterattack needed finesse. This incumbent senator had been re-elected for years with a ten-point margin or more. He ended up winning again that time in 2014, but with only a one-point margin, a huge difference from his margins in the past. We called that a success, although we wondered if a few more dollars there could've gotten his opponent elected instead. There was some fear that damaging reprisals could be coming and that where we once had an opponent now we had an enemy, but in the end that state senator realized that picking a fight on early childhood education was not in his best interest. Like all bullies, he moved on to fight weaker foes.

When you have a brand as well known as STC it cuts through some of the political noise; voters trust an organization more than the self-promotion of candidates and parties. During this time we were also successful in a variety of more positive campaigns, including moving voters toward a Republican South Carolina state school board chair with our endorsement. It took about $100,000 in mailings, radio, and social media advertising. We also aggressively engaged with a progressive Seattle city ballot initiative to make pre-K available to all residents of Seattle and went to work for four intense weeks to shore up the local organizers. Our data clearly showed that our efforts paid off, and we ended up winning with a narrow margin. Conversely, our efforts on behalf of a California congressman in the most expensive race in 2014 didn't seem to do much; Ami Bera, the Democratic incumbent, won, but we couldn't claim any credit as there were too many other groups who were also investing their time and money in the race. This race was won by less than a 1 percent margin and took weeks to recount and certify. And while close elections always reinforce the maxim "every vote counts," it's also true that everyone who contributed shares in that success—no one gets all the credit. SCAN realized that its drop in the bucket helped, but it was not a game changer like the effort we had in the Seattle ballot initiative. After the races were over, we spent about three months looking intently at the data that we had collected. Where did we succeed, where did we fail, and where did the brand just not carry at all? That data helped us create a plan to implement from 2014 to 2016. It was time to take the next step.

As the 2016 election season approached, SCAN employees began engaging with politicians to talk about our two priorities. We needed to find out which politicians would support us and who might oppose us, so we could know where to put our efforts. We were also actively looking to build champions for our causes. We had to find politicians who were willing to take the lead on the issues, not just support them. We knew from our early efforts that localizing our issues made us more effective, and that we also had some very different groups of supporters to balance. We needed to get our diverse groups to make it obvious that they would use our priorities as a reason to support or oppose a candidate for office.

One of our first big successes took place in New Hampshire. We chose to focus on that state for two reasons: they didn't even have mandatory kindergarten, and we knew that every 2016 presidential candidate would be in the state at some point. If we could make early childhood education an important part of the local political scene, the national candidates would be sure to pick it up. A school board or alderman race in the capital city of Manchester with early childhood education as an issue would get big collateral benefits by being noticed by candidates and staffs of presidential campaigns. This is what we call a twofer. We started off by working the school board and alderman races to get candidates to take public positions in support of all-day kindergarten. We asked for pledges and candidate questionnaires, and then we judged who the "kids' candidate" was. In return SCAN offered a sort of seal of approval for who would make good on promises on early education and who would not. We wanted candidates to see an advantage if they got SCAN's endorsement, and we wanted them to see a problem if they didn't. SCAN's endorsement didn't just come with a gold star of approval; it came with candidate support in the form of phone banks, canvassing, paid mail, and advertising. In small races that kind of spending can make a huge difference—and in Manchester, New Hampshire, it did.

After our successes in those smaller races, we scaled up to the mayoral race and finally the gubernatorial race in 2016. While the candidate we supported didn't actually become governor, the Republican victor called Mark Shriver a few weeks after the election to express how impressed he was with our campaign. He then promised to lead the effort to make kindergarten and pre-K available to New Hampshire. This is our theory of change at work: if you run good, effective, credible campaigns on issues, you will get noticed by everyone that matters, even your opponents.

It was now time for us to aim higher, to move from local politics to the national stage. I took our ideas on maternal, newborn, and child survival to the Maternal and Child Health Roundtable, which had been meeting on the issue for many years. We drafted a white paper with the policy concepts written out and backed up by quantifiable data. Our job was to say, You know how these programs can be done better, scaled more quickly, and delivered more efficiently—here is how you can tell Congress to do better. Show them what results can be achieved under your strategy (50 percent reduction in mortality by 2020 and eradication of preventable deaths by 2030). We knew this approach would work, but many nonprofit coalitions that have been together for a long time have a kind of clique mentality—they don't really like newcomers and can tend to disregard their opinions. For as liberal or progressive as many of these organizations are, they are also conservative in their approach to advocacy and especially the rough-and-tumble world of writing a bill and passing it. In this case, not only were we newcomers to the group, but we were coming with a very bold and aggressive approach to the issue and a proposition: it was time for them to write a bill. STC had gotten us an invitation, but our reception was distinctly chilly. Skepticism, cynicism, maybe a little mild contempt could be felt. The group basically told me that what I was proposing was impossible. They couldn't possibly write legislation; that wasn't their job. In the past they had mostly focused on appropriation line items that supported specific programs; they had never before really written any legislation. But this sort of action was the reason Mark and I had created SCAN, and I knew that if we wanted to make a big difference, writing legislation was the way to do it.

Our proposition was quite basic: SCAN had chosen maternal, newborn, and child survival as a priority, so we were going to put our new political muscle behind this issue and write a bill to rally behind. The Maternal and Child Health Roundtable was a well-established coalition of international organizations that had been working on this issue for over a decade. More than fifty organizations were at the table, and we respected the group and the work they'd done over the years. But they had never gone on the offensive with a policy idea. They effectively defended budgets and line items, they worked with USAID on improving program designs, but they hadn't taken the issue to Congress to demand a new and more aggressive approach to addressing their cause. Working from within an existing group is always a bit easier if they welcome the new idea and strategy—the *if* is always a big question mark. Since STC had been part of this roundtable for years, we offered to base our operation and leadership within their organization—an existing coalition of providers and the new political muscle of SCAN for leadership. We also made it clear that if they'd rather not engage, we were prepared to go it alone or find other willing organizations by forming a new coalition for this purpose. I have often found that a train leaving a station has more passengers on it than a train parked on the tracks. Creating urgency can spur action. That was certainly true here, as we did eventually receive the support of the groups in the room.

During the writing of the act I drew heavily on my experiences in PEPFAR and global AIDS. While the goals were different, the overall structure was similar: we needed new program paradigms that could scale with innovative finance provisions. I had the credibility and experience to be able to drive the group. I told Mark we were going to sell them the PEPFAR of maternal newborn child survival. It was a tough process: some members of the group refused to participate, as they thought writing a bill was just too dangerous. Others, however, participated fully, and in due time we were ready to present the Reach Every Mother and Child Act, also known as the Reach Act. The Reach Act seeks to increase efforts in the US to assist developing countries in increasing maternal newborn survival. The goal is to end preventable maternal, newborn, and child deaths by 2035. The act also explains how we will achieve this goal using a mix of public and private financing to deliver proven interventions to improve the health of mothers and their children. These new financing provisions were key, as the current funding situation in the United States does not allow for a traditional budget and appropriations for a new program—we are barely holding on to what we have. We also are faced with Republicans who are not signing on to bills that have been scored by the congressional budget office to cost money. This dynamic requires us to come up with new and innovative ideas that will hopefully gain the support of Republicans to move forward. I had no wish to write a bill that embraced a delusional fiction for funding; I wanted something that could work.

We introduced the bill with bipartisan support to both the House and the Senate in September 2014 as a marker bill, designed to test support. We had a remarkable group of champions from both sides of the aisle, which showed the effectiveness of our strategies throughout the campaign. Having been successful in our test, we then reintroduced the bill again in 2015 with that same level of bipartisan support. In the Senate we had Chris Coons (D-DE), Lindsey Graham (R-SC), and Susan Collins (R-ME); and in the House of Representatives Dave Reichert (R-WA), Michael McCaul (R-TX), Betty McCollum (D-MN), and Barbara Lee (D-CA). Coons was our first and most enthusiastic champion, and he really took the lead to get the bill going. Graham was our original Republican sponsor, but when we reintroduced it in 2015 he didn't co-sponsor—he was running for president and wasn't making commitments to bills that might have a bit of controversy (such as abortion or family planning). Collins stepped in as the lead Republican.

Despite this, we were not quite ready to get it to the floor by the end of that session of Congress, and while I had high hopes for the bill running up to the presidential election in 2016, that election changed the political landscape dramatically. I truly believe that had Hillary Clinton been elected president, our bill would have been on a fast track to her desk. I don't see Donald Trump having the same level of support for our goals, and so we must now adjust our strategy for the years ahead of us. Frankly, our plan is to work around the Trump administration as much as possible, by gaining a broad range of support from Congress and fast-tracking the bill to success. Fast-tracking means the House majority leadership can recommend that a bill be taken up under suspension of the rules, which means it is put on the floor for a straight up or down vote—usually because it's deemed noncontroversial. In the Senate the process is called unanimous consent. This is a privilege of the Senate and allows any senator from any party to object (by voice vote) to moving a bill to the floor for any reason. When senators want to offer amendments to bills or want to stop them, they use this privilege to negotiate opportunity for changes and time for speeches, debates, and amendments. If no senator objects, the bill has unanimous consent. Usually you start in one chamber, pass the bill, and take the exact same bill to the next chamber, where you need to pass it without amendment. It carries by voice votes, but a recorded vote can be requested. Then the bill can go directly to the president for signature, passing conference committees and the need to repeat floor votes once again. The process is a steep hill to climb, but we are trying it now.

Regardless of what the future may bring, I am proud of the work SCAN has done and continues to do in fighting for children worldwide. Working with Mark to create such an innovative group has been very rewarding, and I have been inspired by the efforts of the people at SCAN and STC.

Second View: Mark Shriver

"We want to be the NRA for kids." I have said that line countless times over the last five years. I used it when I participated in a public conversation in front of two hundred people with TV host Willie Geist. Willie smiled and said, "Mark, that is the worst analogy ever!" Everybody laughed. When I say it publicly, the audience usually laughs—nervously. Given today's environment, that nervous laugh is now more charged and poignant, but it is a nervousness we need.

Everybody knows the National Rifle Association—the NRA—and whether you love them or hate them, you know they are influential. Saying that line is a punch in the gut for people who can't stand the NRA and think of themselves as advocates for kids. In fact, one woman told me it was a punch in the gut—and a punch in the face! But that is the point—we all need that figurative punch to wake up and become engaged in the political process on behalf of kids. I'm always very clear that what the NRA stands for, the tactics they use, and the sheer arrogance of their political posturing is abhorrent to me and would never be the framework for our analogous effort at SCAN. But with different tactics and a diametrically opposing value system, I believe we can build a powerhouse political community for kids in the United States. That will not happen unless we take the punch and awaken ourselves to the real politics at play. I believe good will always defeat evil, but good needs to get in shape for the fight—and get in the arena.

After I make that "NRA for kids" statement, I always ask the audience members to raise their hand if they have given money directly to a candidate based on his or her position on kids' issues. Regardless of the size of the crowd, rarely do more than two or three people raise their hands. (Once, five people raised their hand, but three of them were board members of SCAN.) It isn't all about money, but money does matter. Our vision for SCAN was to have all the tools in the toolbox necessary to win in the competitive, high-stakes game of advocacy. In the end, the power is at the ballot box, and we need to have the capacity to make politicians accountable to voters who do prioritize children and the issues that are important to their futures. That will take a fundamental realignment of culture and assets to achieve success, but we started SCAN to do exactly that work. I'm inspired as I write this section in the spring of 2018— look at those Parkland students! I marveled at the March for Our Lives in Washington, DC. Those students and their supporters aren't using the NRA's framework or tactics, but they are using their political assets to the maximum effect—and the cracks in the NRA's power grip are showing. What those students have done is fundamentally political—that's where change happens.

I started SCAN in part because kids don't vote and kids don't give money to politicians. And poor kids' parents don't give money, either. When political deals are being cut, all too often children's needs are not on the table. Simply put, kids don't have a voice in the political process. If the NRA analogy makes you uncomfortable, don't use it. But remember, there's a reason that seniors are a priority, and you don't have to look any further than the AARP. Consider this: The federal government spends $6 on the elderly for every $1 they spend on children. The AARP has political power, just like the NRA does—and just like kids don't.

I was working for Save the Children, a 501(c)(3), when a small group of friends and I hatched the idea of creating SCAN. It was a controversial idea—why would a well-known, well-respected charity delve into partisan politics? Would that shift potentially alienate funders and elected officials who could then cut Save the Children's federal and state grants? Carolyn Miles, the CEO of Save the Children, agreed to review a business plan; if she saw real opportunity, she would take it to Save the Children's board of trustees. We pulled together a top-notch team led by Tom Sheridan. Tom understood policy as well as anyone in Washington, but just as important—if not more so—he understood board politics and politics in general. It's worth underscoring that last line: plenty of folks understand policy, but not many know how to turn policy into legislation that can actually be passed. And plenty of people understand the legal steps to creating a 501(c)(4), but few understand how to navigate the internal dynamics of a board of trustees who need to be convinced to take a risk. It's always easier to just say no—it's hard to create something new, something that might be controversial, something that is unknown.

Tom and his colleagues at the Sheridan Group got us there. SCAN is not the NRA for kids yet, but we are moving in the right direction. As Martin Luther King, Jr., said, "The long arc of history bends toward justice." We are helping to bend that arc, and pretty soon we are going to be the NRA for kids!

TAKEAWAYS

The creation of SCAN was a revolutionary move for Save the Children, one that I suspect will be much copied as time goes on. While Mark and I were confident from the start, there are a few lessons we learned along the way that may be of assistance to someone else attempting a similar feat.

First, don't be afraid to be bold.

When Mark and I first approached the board about creating a 501(c)(4), they were understandably skeptical. However, we worked diligently to convince them that our plan was solid, and we never compromised on our goals. It was incredibly important that SCAN not be sidelined or neutralized by STC, so we wrote a bold plan to make it a successful operation. We tied the success of SCAN directly to the mission of STC—we were the force multiplier for mission-specific goals being achieved.

Second, don't underestimate the value of having specific targets.

STC is a global and enduring operation, and it works in a wide variety of different areas from health to education. It was evident from the beginning that SCAN was not going to be able to function the same way. Getting the board to select a domestic priority and a global priority was crucial in SCAN's ability to succeed. Had we had a broader focus, we would not have been nearly as successful. Convincing groups like this that they can't boil the ocean is tough but critical.

Third, understand the value of nonpartisanship.

Bipartisanship is often thrown around as a magical catchphrase, but in my experience I have found that it can often be detrimental. Groups that try to please both sides of the aisle often end up giving one party the ability to veto an entire effort. From the beginning, SCAN was decidedly nonpartisan, so no one had to wonder what side we were on. We had our two priorities, and we would accept people from either political party if they were willing to work with us in achieving our goals. We were clear that we weren't on either side of their aisle; rather, we created an aisle of our own, and that would determine whether you were good or bad on kids' issues—whether you got thanked or spanked.

Fourth, hire great talent and let them experiment until the data show success.

Those early Senate races right after we formed SCAN were crucial in our later successes. We were able to give our staff the freedom to experiment with ideas—anything they thought would work, we were willing to try. We then followed up with extensive testing to get a real data-driven view of what was successful and what we should abandon. This structure made it easy to capitalize on our successes and move on from tactics that didn't work as well.

KEY QUOTES AND LESSONS

- In politics you must be prepared to both "thank and spank"—if you don't do both, you will quickly become irrelevant.
- Nonprofits must be willing to fully utilize their 501(c)(4)s, not just hide them away.

- Betray conventional wisdom and think bigger.
- Add value instead of introducing competition when entering a new field, especially if you have a new tool.
- Don't let tradition disguise itself as action or allow coalitions to create a lowest common denominator for the goals.

THE THREE P 'S FOR SCAN

Policy: "You can't boil the ocean," as the saying goes. The hardest point in the initial process was narrowing the policy agenda. Choosing issues that would get political and policy attention also requires some awareness of what is possible in the political space. This is often a challenge for large nonprofits; they are usually well known and rely on fund-raising across many issues to meet budget demands, so asking for something as streamlined as two priorities can feel discordant on many levels. For STC (and then SCAN) this was made a bit harder because of their domestic and international development services. I was careful to ensure that they chose their two policy priorities with some eye toward politically relevant issues, issues I was sure I could get some level of bipartisan support for. Especially in the beginning of an operation like a 501(c)(4), you want to set yourself up to win. Once you've won, policy makers and political leaders recognize your capacity and expertise. Then you can take on the harder and more difficult issues, but it's unwise to create policy goals that are too difficult at the start.

Politics: This was the sweet spot Mark desperately wanted to hit. He wanted SCAN to be relevant politically—respected, credible, and effective. But this is not normally or culturally where large nonprofits see their work or mission. Many see political power as antithetical to their mission and work. Finding a comfortable but clearly effective way to build political clout takes time when working with organizations that have never done this work before. The layers of resistance can be encumbering—boards of directors, executive teams, staff, volunteers, donors, and philanthropy all have to be considered and managed as you try to develop a best-in-class nonprofit into a best-in-class advocacy and political operation. Avoiding fear and timidity was essential. Assuring stakeholders that this work was mission focused and would enhance the organization took time and patience. We needed to prove to all of them that by using politics effectively they could achieve their mission, increase their brand identity, and succeed on multiple levels. They needed to be ready to both thank and spank, depending on what the moment needed. This isn't always a pretty business, but it is where change really happens, and you must have the tools to be capable of playing effectively. SCAN is almost four years old, and it is changing this game for the better.

Press: For SCAN, the press has meant a constant push to keep the issues out in the public domain for discussion. We never lacked the support of the general public. Most Americans agree with early childhood education; they just don't prioritize it. It's not the first and most important thing they ask a candidate at a debate, and it's not the thing they use to decide who they'll support. Our job was to know the issues and the messages that worked with voters, so we could keep our goals at the top of their minds. Social media has dramatically changed the equation in this space, and SCAN has really prioritized being omnipresent in social media: active Twitter and Facebook work, and jumping into Instagram as soon as it emerged.

SCAN also mastered the art of collateral benefit—all the activity in Iowa and New Hampshire in 2015 was aimed at school board and statehouse races, but we knew and designed our media attention to capture the presidential candidates that were crisscrossing those states. Buying the small billboards at the luggage carousel in Des Moines was designed to get the attention of candidates and staff—even though the message was about Iowa's children. Running radio spots in Manchester, New Hampshire, to help school board candidates was also aimed at getting into the ears of presidential candidates and staff. Hiring a communications director that knew the political press well was significant. Brendan Daly immediately sent a message to the political press that SCAN was serious and was on the field to win.

CHAPTER 7

Taking America Forward

*"Social entrepreneurs flock like
eagles—they don't"*

DECEMBER 5, 2007. I was stuck in the Denver airport thanks to a weather delay. On a smeary TV screen in the terminal I watched as presidential candidate Barack Obama gave a speech from Cornell College in Iowa, a speech I was supposed to be watching in person. My frustration and annoyance fell away as I heard him say, "That is why I won't just ask for your vote as a candidate; I will ask for your service and your active citizenship when I am president of the United States. This will not be a call issued in one speech or program; this will be a cause of my presidency."

I was floored, and awestruck at the reality of a presidential candidate putting out a platform of ideas that I had created out of whole cloth just a few months earlier. This moment felt like a touchdown in a championship football game. The success was made sweeter by the fact that former senator

Harris Wofford, who until his death in January 2019 was our senior counsel at the Sheridan Group, gave the introduction of Senator Obama. In the speech, Obama urged young Americans to form a new generation of public service, and promised to create a social investment fund network that would bring together public and private sectors to scale up successful programs. It was a powerful speech and an incredible moment for me professionally and personally.

It won't come as a surprise when I say that it took a lot of hard work to get to the point where a candidate for president presents a whole platform you've worked on in a major campaign speech. My involvement in what would become the social innovation platform and then the White House Office of Social Innovation and Civic Participation started before the candidates for the 2008 election had even been selected. In 2006 I attended a conference of social entrepreneurs called the Gathering of Leaders. New Profit, founded in 1998 by Vanessa Kirsch, put on the conference. New Profit is a national nonprofit venture philanthropy fund that seeks to invest in social entrepreneurs to help them grow their impact and develop systematic change.

The term *social entrepreneur* is relatively new. It gained currency thanks to young creative leaders in nonprofit service providers who sought to define a new style and bring discipline to delivering social services. They were dedicated to innovation and to coming up with new ideas to solve old problems. They were committed to stricter standards on data collection, evaluation, and measures of success, and they were challenging traditional government designs and regulations. As a whole they were passionately resolved to change the assumption that social programs were incapable of actually solving problems.

The idea for the Gathering of Leaders was to bring together social entrepreneurs from a variety of different organizations and have them learn from each other. New Profit had invited a huge range of organizations and leaders, from well-known and established groups like Teach for America and Habitat for Humanity to smaller, newer organizations like Public Allies, Year Up, and Youth Villages. The range of social policy topics was impressive—education, civil leadership, health, poverty, immigration, and more—all being addressed at one conference. Usually I don't have the time to go to conferences just to listen, but I had known Vanessa and her husband, Alan Khazei, for years, and Vanessa is not an easy person to say no to. This new breed of social entrepreneurs also intrigued me, and as a social worker I really liked the energy and innovation they were bringing to social policies.

Vanessa and Kim Syman, one of the managing partners, had warned me beforehand that many of the people at the gathering were probably going to be quite skeptical about my presence; many of them believed that government was the antithesis of innovation and looked down on groups that received government money. With that in mind, I spent the first few days of the conference listening and observing, without speaking up at all. Vanessa had commented to me that social entrepreneurs tend to "flock like eagles," which is to say they don't tend to do well with group work. Social entrepreneurs tend to have an alpha personality type: most are interested primarily in their own ideas and are not necessarily cooperative in planning or execution. Vanessa was right about the personality type, but it seemed to me that if these social entrepreneurs could somehow manage to work together, they could be a powerful force. Each day ended with a plenary where people called fire starters would get up and share a new thought, opinion, or idea for the group to contemplate. Some of these fire starters brought up challenging topics, including privilege, the role of faith communities, and ways to change philanthropy as a whole. It made for some fascinating conversations.

As the third day drew to a close, Vanessa and Kim came to me and asked if I would be willing to share my thoughts at the final plenary session. I was concerned that people would react negatively and feel like I had been spying on them, but I did have some thoughts I wanted to share. There were about a hundred people in the room that evening when I stood up to speak, and the message I wanted to deliver was hard-nosed but heartfelt. I began by outing myself: "Ladies and gentlemen, I am a lobbyist." There was an awkward hush. "I came here to listen, but I have been asked to share a few thoughts. I recommend you fasten your seat belts, because what I'm about to tell you is fairly direct but useful, I hope. The American public has lost their trust in social policies and social programs. Too many voters see our social safety net as wasted money with no results. I am impressed by the successes of the people at the conference, but you may never be more successful than you are at this particular moment unless you forge partnerships, especially with public policy and advocacy groups." My point was simple: they would never be able to scale up to a national organization that could actually really address the problem unless they wanted to start working with others. I trusted them and their program data—they were on the ground working in communities every day. I saw the potential political power in restoring confidence in the American taxpayers' commitment to use their hard-earned dollars to solve problems, and I also saw a concrete rationale to change the role of government from provider to catalyst using these new social innovations as the rationale.

But this is my own personal theory of change: in order to actually solve a social problem, you have to change how the government is managing it. Whether that involves designing a new piece of legislation, revamping existing government programs, or developing new sources of funding, advocacy is a crucial part of solving problems, instead of just treating them. It was not the time to really get into the details of what advocacy could achieve for the people gathered, but I proposed a very broad idea to use the 2008 presidential campaign as a way to introduce a new idea for social policy and the role of government: social innovation. I then invited those who were interested to meet me in the back of the room so we could discuss the concept in more detail.

To my surprise, more than half of the participants gathered in the back of the room for a brief brainstorm on how we could develop a policy platform and an advocacy strategy on behalf of these social entrepreneur groups. I hadn't come prepared with any sort of concrete plan, so when Vanessa,

Kim, and I met about a week after the gathering, we agreed that I would work on the basics of a plan. Our job was to create a vision, flesh out ideas for a policy platform, and create a strategy to advance it. If the vision was agreeable, we would then move to a strategic planning process to look at the operational and budget demands, and then we would present our ideas at the gathering the next year. An eleven-month project was off and running with not much more than fifteen minutes of remarks. I checked in with New Profit periodically throughout the next year as I brainstormed ideas for what sort of program would work best for this specific group of people.

One year later, at the same lovely hotel in the Catskill Mountains, we had put together a fully fleshed-out presentation to introduce the work of social entrepreneurs as a new policy platform called social innovation. We proposed to the group that they organize themselves under the name America Forward, which would be a coalition of social entrepreneurs dedicated to advancing a policy agenda in the 2008 presidential campaign. This was bold and audacious. A group of people who one year prior were potentially hostile to the very ideas of advocacy and policy were now being asked to take their maiden voyage in advocacy during a presidential campaign cycle.

I knew this was wild, but I wanted to appeal to their collective innovation and disruption instincts. They were and remain leaders who live by the mantra "go big or go home." Presidential campaigns are not a good venue for beginners to the political process, but they are a unique chance to bring a new idea to rapid fruition, especially if the candidates and the electorate are in a mood for change. I was convinced that 2008 was going to be a change-focused election. Since there was no incumbent, both parties would be presenting new candidates, and it was the perfect venue to really get ideas out there. By this point it was 2007, and the primaries were just getting started. We had to get the ball rolling, and we had to do it quickly.

Over the course of our planning and thinking we realized that it would be incredibly important to be as bipartisan as possible throughout the process of creating our ideas and strategy. We had convinced New Profit to find the resources to bring on a Republican firm to help us, and so I asked Scott Hatch, my Republican counterpart in the ONE Campaign, to join us in the process of creating our ideas.

The next few months were a whirlwind of activity, as we were basically trying to create a campaign from scratch. From the start we had an ambitious goal: we wanted to reimagine the role of government in social services as a catalyst instead of as a provider. Most social policy is created in Washington, often as a response to a crisis or demand from the population. Policy tends to be written from a top-down perspective by bureaucrats who are at a distance from the real issues; rarely are the providers of service in the room when the architecture of policy is created. This results in inflexible, highly constrained rules for delivering services, which tend to make implementation more a function of accounting than of actually addressing human needs. I saw this first-hand when we wrote the Ryan White CARE Act with eight AIDS service organizations at the table—they wrote what they needed from government, namely resources and flexibility; they'd already created the effective program design themselves. I see it every day when foster care programs put rules and reimbursement ahead of the best interests of children and the results are ruined lives, not productive citizens. Our goal was to instead have the federal government work as a partner: investing in the programs that were demonstrating successes and creating competition that would produce more innovation. We wanted to have the government facilitate social entrepreneurs to make more individually tailored programs that could be then scaled up to meet bigger needs. In the end we found very consistent ways to get at both Republicans and Democrats: Democrats like programs that solve problems and help people. Republicans like a "pay for what works," businesslike approach to the process. We deliberately tried to carry those ideological frameworks forward and combine them in one coherent platform of ideas.

At the end of all our brainstorming and planning, we ended up with a menu of options that we wanted to present to the political candidates. They would be able to pick and choose from a huge variety of ideas, from large-scale ones, like creating a new White House office on social innovation or creating a program for mandatory national service (either military or civilian), to smaller things, like encouraging young people working at FEMA to do disaster relief through a program like FEMA Corps, which would recruit, train, and manage young people trained as first responders for disasters. Our ideas had to meet a variety of criteria, but most importantly we wanted to be sure to offer a mix of things that would appeal to both Republicans and Democrats. Now it was time to get to work and present our ideas.

This was all taking place during the primaries, so we asked for a meeting with every candidate who was still in the race. If they said yes, we went to their campaign headquarters and presented them with the menu of options and offered our assistance on figuring out how to make those options a part of their platform. It was very interesting to see which items the different candidates were interested in. John McCain's staff was interested in the idea that everyone should do a year of service: people could choose between the military or public service. Hillary Clinton, on the other hand, was interested in about half the ideas we presented, but balked on those that required bigger government spending. To her credit, she did agree to meet with different social entrepreneurs and national service volunteers at each of her tarmac stops throughout the campaign. We would gather ten or so different social entrepreneurs to meet her when she landed, and each of them would present her with a card with the name of their organization and some data about their role in the community. Gratifyingly, she would often mention these people in her speech later that day. Even Mike Huckabee agreed to have a meeting with us and liked our ideas about using national service in faith-based organizations.

We published a briefing book titled *America Forward: Invent, Invest, Involve.* It was a briefing book for intended candidates and policy makers from all levels of government, but we were really pitching it to the presidentials. Inside the front cover of that book was a map, and every state had no less than two specific agencies listed. Inside the book, each agency on the map had a name and a description of the social innovation they were working on, with results noted. One of my favorites was Youth Villages, one of eleven we cited for Tennessee. They pioneered a transformative foster care approach and went on to be a national model for foster care reform legislation passed in 2010.

But by far the most positive reaction we received was from Barack Obama's campaign. Michelle Obama had previously worked as a social entrepreneur, so she and Barack had a personal connection to the sorts of ideas we were presenting. I was with the group who flew to Chicago to meet the Obama team, and I immediately knew that this campaign was special. Even their office was impressive. I've spent a lot of time working in presidential campaigns, and never had I seen such a professional, clean space (no empty pizza boxes, stale donuts, or weird dirty sock smells). When we got to the conference room, the entire senior-level staff was already there—pollsters, policy wonks, field team—all ready to talk. While most of the other campaigns did see us, those meetings were often short and included mostly lower-level staff with a sprinkling of senior folks who were polite but uninterested. When we offered Obama's staff the menu of options, they immediately told us that this was different. They wanted every option, and they wanted it to be exclusively theirs. We told them that we couldn't give them exclusive access, but if they were interested we would help them launch the ideas. That led to Obama's "A Call to Serve" speech in Iowa, where he laid out his vision around social innovation and national service. Our ideas had been accepted wholeheartedly by his campaign, and I was excited to see what could happen next.

As the presidential election approached, we continued to offer our assistance to the different candidates, and we were thrilled when Obama was elected. He had taken all of our ideas and made them an important part of his campaign platform. People were ready to celebrate, and some were happy to just sit back and enjoy the success. We soon discovered, however, that our successes only meant more hard work. We had worked so hard to create a campaign, but now it was time to pivot to advocacy. We needed to come through with the support we had promised Obama. He had used our ideas on the campaign trail, and now we had to make them happen. This was my first experience with trying to embed something new into an administration: most of my previous advocacy work had involved writing legislation and then letting the administration translate that into offices and grants. Helping to actually launch programs inside a new administration was a whole different ball game.

This was an important stage in the development of America Forward: the switch from a campaign strategy to an advocacy strategy. Presenting ideas to a campaign takes a variety of skills, but doing advocacy work is different. Presenting ideas requires sound research (polling), great talking points, and resources (ideas for events, speeches, photo opportunities, tours of programs, information about key big donors who like your idea). When you pivot to advocacy, you need to put more meat on the bones. We had to begin thinking about how real policy initiatives would be rolled out: in a first hundred days agenda, new bills written and introduced, new agencies developed? Identifying bipartisan champions? Agencies where programs would be housed? Personnel to staff those new agencies and initiatives? There was a laundry list of things to consider when preparing for the pivot to advocacy. Creating real muscle required new skills, capacity, and resources. We were like the dog that chases the bus: we were so busy chasing the bus that when we caught it, we were a little unprepared.

The first thing we needed to do was get a team dedicated to the implementation of Obama's social innovation campaign promises. This was not as easy as it may sound. Candidates makes thousands of promises across every aspect of government domain, so getting your own transition team can be a tall order. The two people most responsible for getting us our own transition team were Melody Barnes, domestic policy advisor to the Obama campaign, and her soon to be deputy Carlos Monje. From early meetings with Melody it was obvious that she understood and embraced the social innovation agenda. She was a delight to work with and an ally—we could not have been successful without her. We had been working with Carlos since the early days of presenting our ideas to the Obama campaign. Carlos had actually been the driving force behind the Iowa speech: he was the domestic policy lead for the Obama campaign (he'd been an Obama Senate staffer). His job was to choose the domestic policy issues and positions that Obama would use to run on and to distinguish himself from the other Democratic candidates in the race. On a cold night, December 5, 2007, at Cornell College in Mount Vernon, Iowa, Barack Obama embraced the social innovation agenda in a speech crafted mostly from Carlos's work.

I was so grateful to Carlos that night. Our roots in the national service movement created a certain trust with Carlos, specifically because a former US senator from Pennsylvania, Harris Wofford, was active on this project and had been an early supporter of Barack Obama. When all was said and done, many people had a hand in the success of the social innovation movement and in America Forward specifically, but Carlos may own the credit for being the core. You'll hear more from Carlos at the end of this chapter.

Once we had our team up and running we were faced with our next big challenge. Obama had agreed to set up the White House Office of Social Innovation and Civic Participation, and now we needed someone to run it. This proved to be more difficult than I could have imagined. All of the social entrepreneurs who were a part of America Forward couldn't give up the causes and organizations they were currently leading in order to go into government work, and we really struggled to find someone who could take the reins. In retrospect we should have been grooming someone for the position throughout the entire campaign, but since we had failed to take that step, we were stuck. We had to widen our search to someone who had not been a part of the process so far, and that made things more difficult.

Eventually we did find a remarkable candidate: Sonal Shah, who was working at Google.org. Sonal had previously worked in the US Department of Treasury before leaving governmental work for the private sector, and she had a deep appreciation for the work of social entrepreneurs. I had not met Sonal until just before she joined the transition team, and I flew to San Francisco when it became obvious she would be moving to DC to join us. It was a fantastic first meeting. Sonal is warm, gracious, humble, and wicked smart. I immediately knew that under her leadership our initiatives and promises would be wisely translated into real initiatives and policy. Sonal is the kind of leader who works hard, seizes opportunities, and understands the rough-and-tumble world of politics. She and Melody had a strong and trusting relationship, which was immensely helpful in those early days.

After we brought in Sonal, Michele Jolin was asked to join the transition as deputy. Michele had been at the Center for American Progress, heavily involved in social innovation for two years at that point. I had kept up a very steady communication with Michele throughout the campaign, and she became an incredible asset. Michele was really our think tank; she had previously done some really excellent work on policy, and her time at CAP gave her extensive resources and political clout with the new administration. They had even produced a book for the transition with some great white papers on various aspects of social innovation.

With Sonal as director and Michele as the deputy, the office began to come together. The combination of Sonal's mature leadership style and Michele's tenacious commitment to the goals of advancing social innovation made for a tremendous team. They worked in tandem, always aware of the other's strengths and conscious of weaknesses that could create trouble. It was not an easy job—indeed, it was full of challenges and setbacks—but both women worked incredibly hard to get everything going. As the Obama team settled into the White House, we needed America Forward to hit the Hill and start working on legislation and appropriations. Campaign promises mean nothing if you can't get them up, running, funded, and authorized in Congress. By April 21 we had written and passed the Edward M. Kennedy Serve America Act, which codified nearly all of our America Forward platform ideas. It was President Obama's second signing ceremony, and it was a wonderful moment for us—we were able to bring both social innovation and national service together in one successful bill.

Perhaps the hallmark idea was the Social Innovation Fund, a new "shark tank" for social entrepreneurs who were willing to bring their best programs and ideas forward with strong evidence that government could scale the intervention with funding. This highly competitive national effort would award no less than $5 million for five years to the winning applications. The idea was simple: let government act as the catalyst for competition among those doing the most impactful work in our communities. The SIF was highly successful for five years but faded into oblivion when the Obama administration came to an end and the advocacy efforts within this community neglected to take the ball forward effectively.

I continued to work with America Forward for three years after the transition, and they were some tough years. As with many movements and campaigns there comes a time when the maturation of the movement hits a transitional moment; for America Forward, this came about a year after we had transitioned to a Hill-based strategy. It was clear to me that America Forward needed to begin to evolve into an independent organization (with a governing board and organizational capacity to grow), or it would hit its limitations very soon. The time had come for a sort of a trade association for the social entrepreneur movement to emerge. However, at that point America Forward was still a wholly owned subsidiary of New Profit, and I believed that fact was limiting its potential. We were seeing the evidence of this in many places: an unwillingness of funders to invest in the work if it was through New Profit, a suppression of leadership for those in competition with New Profit leaders, and political assets we could not utilize because New Profit controlled America Forward 100 percent and more organizations could not engage. Over the next few months I tried to create conversations about how America Forward could become a more independent organization, but frankly those conversations were not successful. At one point Michele and I even flew to Boston to meet with Vanessa to discuss merging America Forward with a new social innovation group that Michele was starting called Results for America, but Vanessa was not interested. To this day America Forward remains a subsidiary of New Profit, focusing only on leaders within New Profit's portfolio. The problem was a common one, based on a cult of personality centered around one leader. In the end, this limited the organization's maturation and growth.

There is some sadness in these facts, but there are also some clear lessons that are helpful for change agents to understand. For one, I will never lead another strategy with this level of ambition without at least a notion of what is needed if we win. In addition, not all movements are destined to become institutions: some have great potential but then expire too soon. America Forward is an example of a wonderful campaign built on hope, change, and innovation that was not able to sustain itself into an institution for a variety of reasons. If I had to do it all over again, I would have split my focus once we had formed our transition team: in addition to building our lobbying and advocacy on Capitol Hill, I would have put more of a focus on organizational development. I was limited at the time by my role as a consultant. I can only work on what my client wants me to focus on, and in this case my client was not interested in what I had suggested as a strong path forward.

Unfortunately, this meant that America Forward was

never able to achieve the successes I had hoped for. The so-cial innovation agenda as it was envisioned is unlikely to evolve in the near future, and the programs we designed will be dismantled and trashed. Our relationship ended on a disappointing note. It was a textbook case of founders syndrome, in which a charismatic leader with outstanding ideas can't cede enough control to let a movement of their own creation grow and flourish. Despite this, I do think the changing role of government as a catalyst has taken root; we continue to make progress on using evidence-based pro-grams to push for bigger social change. Our ideas continue to be discussed by both sides of the aisle on Capitol Hill, and I remain hopeful. An interesting point to be made here is that in a functioning democracy nothing is permanent; all things can change. The fight is never really over if you are committed to making a lasting difference. Windows of op-portunity open and close, and you need to be ready to adapt and modify your strategy in order to seize the moment.

Second View: Carlos Monje

The 2008 Obama campaign was the most exhausting, exhilarating, and inspirational thing I've ever been a part of. Over those two years, I worked ridiculous hours, made lifelong friends, met my wife, and wit-nessed a long-shot presidential bid blossom into a national movement powered by everyday people.

Campaign policy teams are a mad scramble—answering questions from precinct captains, writing fact sheets, and working on debate prep. I first met Tom Sheridan in a high-rise campaign conference room, where he pitched a well-researched national service proposal that included the crazy idea that government could help find and scale ideas that worked. I was impressed and told my bosses so.

I soon got word that Obama wanted to deliver a service speech. Like I had done many times before, I scrambled to put a policy paper together. I used America Forward's blueprint as a base and added the candidate's own touches. Weeks before the Iowa caucuses, Senator Obama gave the speech, and he was introduced by the legendary Harris Wofford. The rest of the campaign that year is well known. I spent the last weeks of the campaign in the swing state of Colorado, and when I got back to HQ on Friday, I was told I had to report to duty on the transition the following Monday.

Presidential transitions are the moment when the poetry of campaigning clashes with the prose of governing. That Monday, I joined the sweaty hordes of campaign staff who invaded DC—bone tired, but eager to change the world. I wanted to be part of the newly established White House Office of Social Innovation, because I had grown to care about the issue.

The service coalition was strong, longtime cross-aisle partners Ted Kennedy and Orrin Hatch had reintroduced the Serve America Act, and everything was gaining momentum.

Following the inauguration, I was tapped to lead negotiations with congressional staffers on the bill. Over the course of several hectic weeks, we went back and forth between House and Senate staff, informed by the incredible team at the Corporation for National and Community Service (CNCS). The most poignant moment came as the bill was nearing final passage. I was squirreled away in the vice president's ornate office in the Senate when we got word that Senator Hatch was renaming the bill to honor his friend Edward M. Kennedy, a touching tribute to the liberal lion of the Senate. Not too long after, I was present as President Obama signed the bill at a DC school surrounded by the legislators and service community leaders who had championed the bill. He handed the signing pen to Kennedy, who was leaning on a cane but smiling broadly.

From when I first met Tom Sheridan in Chicago and through the signing of the bill and the subsequent implementation, he was always ready with advice, political intelligence, and, importantly for a young staffer, encouragement. America Forward's strategy took years to develop and implement. It was

> multifaceted and resilient. The Obama campaign and White House put a lot of elbow grease into the effort, but without Tom, we'd still be complaining about the need to reauthorize the CNCS.

TAKEAWAYS

When I first started talking to the social entrepreneurs at that 2006 Gathering of Leaders, they were apprehensive about getting into advocacy. They viewed the government as a polluting factor and were sure that they were doing better work because they were not accepting governmental funds. Yet by 2008 we were in the White House, instituting a new office and a fund devoted solely to helping social entrepreneurs. It took a lot of hard work to get there, and I learned some very important things along the way.

First, it is incredibly important to know your moment.

While many people thought it was crazy to take a group of people who were totally new to advocacy and throw them into a presidential campaign, we knew it was the best way to get our ideas out there. There was no better time to present an entirely new set of ideas than in such an open setting, and our successes proved we were correct to take such a gamble.

Second, strong early leadership is crucial in uniting a group.

Vanessa and Kim were willing to put in the money and the time right from the start, which gave me the ability to create a platform I was comfortable presenting to the other social entrepreneurs. They also created the setting, the Gathering of Leaders, without which none of this would have been possible. These two different but strong leaders were able to provide a valuable opportunity for these successful people to band together and make a real difference at a policy level.

Third, there is value in a willingness to just listen.

America Forward would not have been created had I not gone to the Gathering with the express intention to just listen, and then when the moment came those social entrepreneurs were willing to listen to me. Further on down the line, the campaigns of the presidential candidates were willing to listen to our menu of ideas around service. Each time someone was willing to take some time and listen to our ideas, we became more successful, until we eventually ended up in the White House.

Fourth, the fight doesn't end when your ideas get accepted.

When Obama was elected, many people at America Forward wanted to stop and celebrate, thinking that we had achieved all of our goals. In reality, the hard work was just beginning, and while we did our best to create a lasting institution, we did not end up succeeding. In politics, nothing is ever really over; the wins of yesterday can become the losses of tomorrow without stewardship, vigilance, and leadership.

KEY QUOTES AND LESSONS

- Coalitions can be created even when trying to unite those who flock like eagles.
- When seizing political opportunity, be aware that there is a pendulum of change, and you need to be nimble and thoughtful about managing the swing.
- When a window of opportunity opens, jump through it! If you'd done a little preparation in advance you're better off, but don't wait when you see your chance. Your opportunity might never come back.
- Wise leadership requires a stubborn focus on the necessities of winning, but it also looks farther down the field to prepare for success and failure. Keep at least one eye on the future.

THE THREE P'S FOR AMERICA FORWARD

Policy: Our initial effort was a challenge: take a concept called social innovation and a group of leaders who described themselves as social entrepreneurs and create a meaningful policy platform on which to unite them and present it to candidates for president in

2008. Defining terms and translating innovative programs into concrete policy ideas was time-consuming
and at times extremely difficult. When we were able
to produce the *America Forward: Invent, Invest, Involve* (written by Shirley Sagawa and Deb Jospin)
briefing book for candidates for president, we were
relieved. We'd crossed a critical threshold for political
success: providing candidates and campaigns something to be for (or against). This first act of defining
policy is critical—especially when charting new terri-
tory or bringing new ideas to the policy and political
debate. This platform of ideas, concepts, and initiatives required a fair amount of effort to ensure it was
bipartisan, truly national in scope, and grounded in
examples and evidence that established the agenda
as credible upon first introduction. I was particularly
proud of the menu approach we used. Not only could
we provide an expansive set of ideas, but we could tai-
lor our list to the continuum of political ideologies
present at the start of the 2008 presidential campaign.
In the end, this platform also gave us a measurement
of our success: Which ideas took off for what candidates? Did those candidates really amplify the platform? Were they successful in proposing the new
ideas? Did the media and public respond well? These
questions were answered as we tracked the ideas
throughout the election, and our success was clear
when the winning Obama campaign team adopted
our ideas wholeheartedly.

Politics: The political power of America Forward was a combination of our use of both local programs and specific leaders as examples of social innovation at work across America. No matter where a candidate was from or the state they were in for a primary, we tried to have examples and leaders available for them to see and use. Putting real voters behind issues and movements is the most effective way to earn your way into a politically relevant position, especially if you're using election campaigns as your vehicle. America Forward also had a number of assets at the elite level that helped us gain traction and credibility early in the process. David Gergen, a presidential advisor and CNN commentator, led the press conference announcing America Forward; he was bipartisan, well known, and well respected, which helped us give a serious impression. Some of the leaders in the social innovation space had made reputations in national elite circles: Michael Brown of City Year and Wendy Kopp of Teach for America are great examples. A number of the organizations that were created by social entrepreneurs had active Democratic and Republican big donors on their boards, and we used those relationships to connect with campaigns. Last, but very important, we had people like Harris Wofford in our corner who were willing to do a good deal of brokering to get our ideas heard. Harris was on the front lines of the social policy revolution of the 1960s and 1970s, and his endorsement of the social innovation platform for the twenty-first century was powerful. His relationship with Senator Obama, early endorsement of our ideas, and continued advocacy with his senior staff all propelled our agenda politically. Timing matters in politics, and America Forward proposed that this was an ideal time politically to introduce new ideas for social policy. The national mood for change isn't always the same, and knowing that there was going to be a resonant message of "hope and change" was an early and important factor in our success.

Press: In all progressive social causes I work on, money and resources can be hard to come by. In this case, we were lucky that the leadership and board of New Profit saw this as an important investment and provided money to build a communications capacity into the very beginnings of the campaign rollout. Just having the launch at the National Press Club in Washington, DC, was a statement of our intention to be relevant as an idea worthy of a presidential campaign. But hiring the right people was the key to the press success of America Forward. We didn't hire your typical PR consulting firm; we hired political communications professionals who were well known and seasoned from previous presidential campaigns. Not only was their work superior, but they also had a network of people who were important and relevant to the decisions that made us successful. Perhaps for the first time in my professional experience, I got to work with political communications professionals like Erik Smith and Stephanie Cutter from the very start of our efforts. Anyone can write press releases, place ads, or work on social media, but knowing where and when and to whom to direct those tactics requires experienced pros, and we had them for this campaign.

CHAPTER 8

Voices for National Service

"All politics is local; make it count at home"

ON A SEPTEMBER day in 2010, I stood in front of a room of volunteers, all of whom had come to DC for the Voices for National Service (VNS) Capitol Hill Day. These volunteers hailed from nearly every state in the union. Some were alumni of AmeriCorps programs; others were board members of well-known service powered organizations like Habitat for Humanity, City Year, or Teach for America. Some were on the staff of programs that depend on Senior Corps—like Meals on Wheels. It was a very diverse group, but everyone in the room had either been in a service program or was connected to the power of national service through their work or volunteer activity. I had been asked to inform, motivate, and inspire these people and help them to successfully pass our message on to their members of Congress. As I told them that day, "Your members of Congress are much more interested in your thoughts than in mine. I'm a lobbyist, but you are constituents—that's where the power comes from, your ability to vote for or against them." The room was full of active, passionate voters, and we needed to be able to harness that power for our cause. I ended by telling them that change begins with individuals, and that only they could achieve the changes they sought—it was up to them to make a difference.

I was not yet working for VNS. I thought that my job that day would be just to fire up the advocates as a favor for a friend and then move on. But once that friend, AnnMaura Connolly, a leader in the social entrepreneur movement and president of VNS, had me invested in the cause, I couldn't turn back. We had not gathered for an easy task: our main message to be delivered on Capitol Hill that day was to push back against a recent Republican House budget proposal that zeroed out the Corporation for National and Community Service (CNCS)—the agency that runs AmeriCorps, Senior Corps, VISTA, and other national service programs. The Republicans were in the minority—though that would soon change after the 2010 midterms—but we still wanted to push back hard against their proposal to make our point. This wasn't a fight about how big we could grow our funding; this was a fight against a party that was ideologically opposed to the government having a role in serving communities. Their slogan was "national service is paid volunteerism," which was false and frankly quite wounding to the hundreds of millions of people who had served and been served by CNCS programs. It was time to show Congress what CNCS was really about.

CNCS was established in 1993 and has six priorities: disaster services, economic opportunity, education, environmental stewardship, healthy futures, and support of veterans and military families. CNCS came about during the Clinton administration, but the idea of harnessing the power of civilian workers was not new. There is a long history of such service in the United States, from the beginnings of Roosevelt's Civilian Conservation Corps in 1933 to the establishment of the Peace Corps in 1961. More recently, President George H. W. Bush had created an Office of National Service in the White House after his inaugural address in 1989, calling for a "new engagement in the lives of others, a new activism, hands-on and involved, that gets the job done." On the morning of Bill Clinton's inauguration, George H. W. Bush asked him to keep and grow the national service idea, and Clinton in turn asked George W. Bush to do the same. This passing of the torch is remarkable and bipartisan, and to me it shows that on the highest political level there is real consensus that this is a program that embodies the values of being American.

Yet despite this bipartisan idea of citizenship in service, CNCS has come under various attacks from Republicans from its inception. It has often been called a permanent boot camp for Democratic organizers, and that first poison pill has never been fully expelled from the politics of CNCS. The Republican House budget was just another battle in a war that had been fought for years.

I spoke to those eager volunteers early on in my involvement with VNS, and little did we know the challenges we would face in the upcoming years. VNS was founded in 2003 as a coalition of national and local service programs that were all seeking to increase support for CNCS as well as increase its budget. VNS is an outside organization that advocates on Capitol Hill and with the administration for budgets and appropriations to grow CNCS programs and improve its mission. My involvement with VNS started in 2006, when I began my work with America Forward. A major player in the America Forward coalition was City Year, and they are arguably the largest and most well-known national service agency in the nation. In fact, the idea of AmeriCorps was inspired by a visit from Governor Bill Clinton (then a candidate for president) to City Year's original program in Boston. I linked Bono up with City Year because I wanted him to connect with a US organization doing work in Africa on AIDS. That allowed me to get to know Alan Khazei and his wife, Vanessa, with whom I worked to create America Forward.

City Year has led the VNS coalition since its inception under the auspices of the indefatigable and brilliant AnnMaura Connolly, who you'll hear from at the end of this chapter. AnnMaura is the senior vice president at City Year and with CEO and founder Michael Brown represents one of the most thoughtful, strategic, and politically sophisticated nonprofit leaders in the nation today. After successfully guiding the ideas of America Forward to victory in the 2008 presidential campaign, I worked side by side with AnnMaura to get the Edward M. Kennedy Serve America Act drafted and passed in time for President Barack Obama to sign it as his second bill and to have Senator Kennedy on hand for the last public signing ceremony of his life. The act was both the authorization of the social innovation agenda we advanced with America Forward and a reboot of the national service movement, a way to mature it and create a new twenty-first-century design for national service.

Our partnership and friendship were firmly in place from our time working with America Forward, but AnnMaura knew the VNS needed a little more special attention—a reset on strategy and tactics as they approached the opportunity of Obama and the opposition of the Republican leadership, notably Paul Ryan, then chair of the Budget Committee and soon to be Speaker of the House. I was still working with America Forward, and I saw a very exciting opportunity to be involved simultaneously on both projects. Social innovation was redefining the role of government, and I saw national service as the human capital pipeline to grow the best ideas in social innovation to scale. There was a lovely vision that, taken together, these two ideas would and could reshape social policy in the twenty-first century, and I wanted to be a part of that.

After the midterm elections of 2010, it became obvious that AnnMaura was right to be a little worried. Paul Ryan's proposed budget actually zeroed out the entire CNCS—they would get no funding from Congress whatsoever. Unlike the budget zero from that first Capitol Hill Day, this one really mattered. Looking back, this was ironically to our benefit: we didn't have to explain to anyone how the budget was going to hurt them. Zero is a very clear message, so we were able to go right into full-scale defense mode. This was the height of the Tea Party movement, and when I went to meet with AnnMaura, I told her we needed to go local. The Tea Party had sprung up as a grassroots organization, and we needed to meet them there. We needed to get out into the communities of the Tea Party people and show them how CNCS was helping their neighbors.

This was a completely novel idea for VNS. They had previously relied on what I call elite-ball politics, calling in big-name allies to save them from one problem or another, including regular attacks from Republicans in Congress. President Clinton fought and won the first battles, and then champions like Senator Ted Kennedy put up powerful firewalls in the Senate to stop Republicans from tearing it down. The game changed dramatically with the rise of the Tea Party; Democratic majorities in the House and Senate were lost, and with those losses the protections we relied upon were weakened. It's worth sharing that Bill Clinton originally proposed AmeriCorps at the urging of George H. W. Bush— a fact that frequently is conveniently forgotten. Republicans pounced on it then as a "boot camp for Democratic campaign operatives." Tea Party budget cutters have taken over the Republican Party and frequently target domestic spending; CNCS is always on the list for cuts, with a justification that the US "should not pay for volunteers." But VNS was started in the early 2000s when George W. Bush was brought to the White House on a wave of fiscally conservative Republicans in the House and Senate.

We soon realized we had a big challenge to address before we could even start our advocacy campaign: no one really knew what CNCS was nor did they really understand what AmeriCorps did, never mind Senior Corps, VISTA, or the Conservation Corps. Our labels were too varied and the brand was so diffused that its impact was not commonly visible or valued. This had a direct effect on how quickly we could localize our advocacy strategy.

What we eventually came up with was what we called the Intel model. Basically, almost all of today's computers, PCs and Macs alike, use chips created by Intel. We wanted to go into these congressional districts and show people everything that was powered by CNCS: Teach for America, Habitat for Humanity, Meals on Wheels. All of these valuable programs benefited from CNCS, but no one knew it. People knew the names of the programs; we just needed to show them that they were all part of a bigger brand. Our job was to make sure people in Congress knew just how much CNCS was giving their community, and we needed to do it quickly.

To make matters slightly more complicated, Republican opposition to CNCS had resulted in a blanket ban on active national service members, such as AmeriCorps members, engaging in any political or advocacy efforts. Republicans feared the program was a training program for Democratic campaign operatives and had won statutory prohibitions on advocacy activity. Service members are allowed to vote, but that is it; they are completely barred from participating in anything political. The regulations are quite strict, and programs that have pushed the boundaries have been caught, defunded, and publicly held up by Republicans as evidence for eliminating CNCS. This, to me, is a First Amendment issue, but it was clearly not the time to fight that battle. We were in a tough spot; VNS's best assets are clearly the people serving local communities, but we were unable to use them. Instead, we were going to have to rely on program alumni, friends and families of corps members, and board members of organizations with AmeriCorps grants. The staff and boards of organizations where CNCS programs were operating had to do the tough and important work of directly advocating for the programs with members of Congress—specifically those members whose districts have programs served by CNCS funding. This patchwork of support would have to be quickly woven together if we were going to make any progress.

In order to determine where we should focus our efforts, we decided our targets should be every congressional district that had an AmeriCorps program and a member of Congress we thought was reachable. We eliminated the hard right Tea Party members for two reasons: we weren't going to change their minds, and we didn't want to show our hand because we wanted an element of surprise. That left us with

411 offices that we wanted to target during the Easter recess, and we wanted to have at least five people in each of those offices telling a story, five people in each office saying, "If you close down CNCS tomorrow, here is what our community would lose."

We encouraged the volunteers to include some theater. We had them bring pictures of people working in soup kitchens or building houses, we wanted them to call the press, make a big deal out of what they were doing. If their representative wouldn't meet with them, we encouraged them to go to town hall meetings and stand up and talk there. Anything we could do to bring attention to the role of CNCS, we did. One creative group put up a billboard in Janesville, Wisconsin—Paul Ryan's hometown—with a photo of Paul and another of a group of AmeriCorps volunteers with a headline that read: "Paul Ryan expects to be paid $174,000 a year for his public service but wants AmeriCorps members to be paid $0 for their service."

My favorite anecdote from this campaign came from Montana. A group of Senior Corps members who worked in a soup kitchen organized themselves to show up in the local district office of Denny Rehberg, the Republican chairman of the House Appropriations subcommittee in charge of funding CNCS. They brought the large wooden soup spoons used to make vats of soup in a senior center in Helena, Montana. The visual prompted the local paper to photograph them, and their picture ended up on the front page of the local paper. Their message clearly got passed to their representative: he never went back to his position of zeroing out

CNCS—in fact his chairman's proposal fully funded Senior Corps. These women had made it very clear that it would be bad for their representative to be seen opposing them. This was local activism at its best: what politician wanted to be seen opposing such a wonderful group of senior citizens?

We created that sort of noise in all 411 offices during the Easter recess, and we scared enough politicians that CNCS ended up with only a small budget cut. It was a remarkable achievement. VNS heard directly from many congressional offices about the tremendous impact that had resulted from our local efforts. I was tired, but proud. We had worked hard, and we had made a difference on our own. It is always a risk to take a well-established group like VNS and change its strategic position and its culture. I was very aware throughout the process that if we lost it would all be on my shoulders, but I knew that if we won we would create a much more powerful group. In politics generally there is no second place; there is no consolation prize or Miss Congeniality sash. I had spent much of the campaign in a state of excited anxiety mixed with a deep sense of responsibility, and now I was finally able to relax. VNS had successfully developed a ground-level model, and our tactics had been successful.

Honestly, we had hoped for some more support from the White House. We asked if President Obama could do an event with some national service groups, and we had hoped for more prioritization in the presidential budgets, but they were in the midst of the economic crisis and were unable to give us the support we wanted. It was a bittersweet moment; our successes came just as our hopes for a national service-focused White House began to disappear. After our first success the White House called a meeting of organizations that were in trouble with the Republican budget proposals and used VNS as their prototype for what effective advocacy looked like. We were proof that localizing efforts was the only viable way to survive the first attack by the Tea Party. We had succeeded without their support, and they were hopeful that others could as well.

In hindsight, a number of things contributed to the success of VNS, but in no small part it was that zero that set us on the path. A zero requires no analysis—everyone knew immediately this was a big and important fight. We had a common enemy that we could use to rally everyone. The threat was so serious that it also created a need for a change in tactic. My mother was fond of the saying "necessity is the mother of invention," and in this case it was 100 percent true. We needed to get away from the elite strategy and rapidly build a field strategy to localize the politics and fight back effectively. I think the shock of the zero snapped the community of national service participants and program providers out of a sense of complacency, in which they didn't really care much about the big picture of budgets and advocacy but only about their own slice. When the whole pie is stolen or it never gets baked at all, everyone loses. That first big fight was, in a way, the easiest part. If we couldn't change the zero, we were doomed. Yet the fight was far from over.

I frequently tell clients that an effective first strike is valuable in and of itself, but it also sends a clear message that you aren't an easy target. In many cases this affords a certain level of protection from the anti-government spending bullies who know how to come after you but rarely are prepared for you to retaliate in kind. Yet it is extremely important that you not falter after that first strike. You must be prepared to continue the fight. After that year of intensity we worked on maintaining a strong local presence, and that's what VNS continues to do today.

It is not possible for any organization or group of grassroots activists to maintain such an intense level of effort as we did in that first blitz of all 411 offices, so instead we have moved to a focused strategy on top-tier targeted districts, which we began in 2014. Every year we select five congressional districts, two Democratic and three Republican, and focus specifically on those areas. These members of Congress are all on the subcommittee that funds CNCS; we focus on the subcommittee because if we win there, we largely just need to hold on for the remainder of the process. As budget and appropriations bills move forward we do engage the larger community, but the intense activity gets focused on those five primary targets each year.

Within those five districts we try to get in touch with every person who has worked for a CNCS group and every board member who is willing to engage with us, and we spend a year training them and teaching them how to create a relationship with their member of Congress. We basically ran a desk operation out of our office, holding regular meetings with leaders in each of those five districts. We set up activities, help them develop scripts for meetings, and coach them on their agendas. When we are finished with the year, we have a trained cadre of people and leaders who can sustain our efforts and maintain a deep relationship with their member of Congress, always reminding them of the power of CNCS. Every local person we train and every Ameri-Corps alumnus who wants to share their passion with their member of Congress is one more person who can make national service a priority in years to come.

This is the future of VNS: harnessing that local capacity and beginning to build a millennial voting bloc. Millennials will control the future of our country, and VNS is trying to make national service a relevant issue to them. We have spent a lot of time thinking about this recently: What does national service look like to millennials? Is it important to them? What can we do to make national service an important voting issue for them? Our initial research on these questions is favorable and lends itself to creating this message platform and a campaign to distribute it. Millennials are more socially progressive, more globally invested, more socially active, and more willing to invest in their communities and the wider world around them. These are great qualities for a future voting bloc that could carry national service to its next level of government engagement. If we are able to make a millennial tradition of supporting national service, that value is sustainable from 2020 to 2060, as millennials will be 60 percent of the voting population over those forty years. We are trying to set up a situation where hopefully both, but at least one, political party will include a robust national service vision in their platform to attract millennial voters. If we can do that, national service can become a sustainable political force.

Second View: AnnMaura Connolly

Voices for National Service was founded in 2003 after the national service community faced significant proposed cuts to funding for AmeriCorps. Misleading arguments about paid volunteering and government mismanagement threatened CNCS, which had become a vital source of resources for organizations facing mounting challenges in underresourced communities across America.

We needed to organize ourselves and come together to make the case for the federal investment and connect the dots between that investment and communities across the country. We needed an ongoing presence in Washington instead of scrambling when crises arose. And we did. In 2003 we worked with colleagues across the field to organize one hundred hours of consecutive citizen testimony on the Hill, offering people who worked in community programs a chance to share their story about what national service meant to them. Corporate CEOs, university presidents, leaders of faith-based and com-

---

munity groups, and governors and mayors across the political spectrum told stories that illuminated the critical role of the federal investment in service in communities large and small, rural and urban, across the country. Editorial boards from the *New York Times* to the *Houston Chronicle* and across the country weighed in. Thousands of citizens came to Washington by bus, train, or car to tell their inspiring stories of service and impact during our citizens hearing. We invited the members to testify, too. We worked together to earn the highest appropriation ever for domestic service programs for the next year. And that was the beginning of VNS.

I first met Tom Sheridan during the Democratic convention in Boston in 2004, which nominated John Kerry for president and introduced the nation to a young candidate for a Senate seat in Illinois, Barack Obama. I was not attending the convention but was in Boston because of my work at City Year. Tom was there at the convention with Bono, and brought him to the City Year headquarters to meet with our AmeriCorps members, staff, and champions. I was struck by the rock star but also by Tom's ability to convince diverse groups to work together around a common mission, as I learned he had done with a divisive and disparate set of cancer groups. It was clear that Tom had a natural skill at building a cohesive movement, and I knew we needed those skills to help us build a strong coalition at VNS. Tom knew how to build a case and engage, and he did it all with discipline and sophistication.

In 2009, VNS and our colleagues across the field worked together on the Edward M. Kennedy Serve America Act, which was a labor of love led by Senators Hatch and Kennedy. The act passed with significant bipartisan support in 2009 to increase funding for CNCS. It was a remarkable achievement on the part of the national service community, and it paved the way for a significant ramping up of national service. Members of Congress on both sides of the aisle came together to craft a visionary piece of legislation that focused on scaling national service in the areas where it was having the most significant impact. We made it clear that national service was something that mattered on both sides of the aisle and for all citizens. We also knew that if more Americans were given an opportunity to serve, it would go a long way toward uniting Americans to address the problems facing their communities and the country.

Despite the passage of that landmark legislation, national service continued to face strong headwinds, not just preventing the expansion of national service but also threatening our ability to maintain current funding levels. We began to work with the Sheridan Group and our colleagues across the national service movement to engage more deeply with congressional decision makers, to focus on building relationships and on the ground, in communities where national service members served. Tom played an essential role in helping us educate our coalition members about the urgency of building strong relationships. Tom helped us understand that members of Congress on both sides of the aisle needed to understand the consequences of their decisions and what would be lost if funding for national service were to be cut or disappear.

For too long, the national service movement had relied on the White House and a handful of congressional champions to help us get over tough spots. Because our system of national service relies on hundreds of nonprofits to recruit and deploy members for their service, we now needed to ask those nonprofits to help members of Congress understand how the federal investment made a difference in the communities they represented. We needed to take our message local. Members of Congress needed to understand that CNCS funding was not just a nice thing; it was necessary in their home community.

Together we worked to train a network of leaders to establish VNS chapters in states represented by members of Congress with decision-making authority over funding for CNCS. This new program designed and deployed a range of advocacy tactics, including in-district site visits, letters to the editor, op-eds, and the activation of key community leaders. As a result of this effort and other grassroots outreach, not only did Congress reverse its originally proposed cuts to national service, but it actually increased funding for CNCS in fiscal year 2016.

Tom is as good as it gets in terms of understanding the political process, and we make a good team of yin and yang. I appreciate how he pushes people to move way beyond their comfort zone when it's required—and that's not infrequently when you're trying to build movements for powerful change.

TAKEAWAYS

My work with VNS has shown me the true power of local politics and clearly demonstrated the issues that come from public funding. We were able to avoid budget cuts year after year because of a few key lessons.

First, if you are dependent on public dollars, you need to be involved in politics.

When you rely on public funds for your organization, your longevity is tied to the election cycle. Elections have consequences, and those consequences spill directly into budget battles or policy fights that can and do threaten the existence of vital programs and services. VNS learned this the hard way after the midterm elections in 2010; in order to fight to keep their funding they needed to get involved in politics, and they needed to do it quickly and effectively.

Second, go back to the base and don't get distracted.

In the stressful time that followed the release of Ryan's budget, it would've been easy to get distracted by the idea of a large national campaign—maybe we should put an ad in the *New York Times*, or maybe we should try to call in some of our big-name allies, like former Presidents Bush and Clinton. Instead, VNS recognized the local power harnessed by Tea Party members, and we quickly worked to use that power ourselves. Having local constituents meet with their members of Congress may seem like a small move, but we proved it could be incredibly successful. We didn't ignore the support of the former presidents, and we did indeed use them in our fight, but we didn't rely on them to power our whole campaign.

Third, never underestimate the power of theater.

Those senior citizens with soup spoons made a difference. Congressman Rehberg saw that article in the paper and realized it would not be good to have his name listed as leading an effort to oppose those women and take food from hungry seniors. The ability to turn a simple office visit into an event covered by the press can be incredibly valuable. A powerful picture on the front page of the newspaper gets the attention of thousands of people and multiplies the message. That is relevant to any politician.

Fourth, elections have consequences, but so do budgets.

When you are in a budget fight, don't justify your programs by talking about billions of dollars or millions of people and programs—the volume undermines the impact. We worked hard to personalize the consequences: 2,500 kids in our middle schools won't have a reading tutor; 175 senior citizens in our community won't get a hot meal delivered. These are real people in real communities. Politicians don't want to be held personally accountable for these types of consequences. Personalize, localize, politicize—that's a formula that has real impact.

KEY QUOTES AND LESSONS

- Powered by CNCS—(the Intel model): recognize your problem and solve it as best you can.
- Be careful not to overbrand. Too many organizations made it hard to know who was doing the work and why it mattered.
- When in crisis, think out of the box and break from tradition. Just because something worked ten years ago

doesn't mean it will work now—in fact, it most likely won't.

- When hit hard, hit back hard. The tendency of nonprofits to shy away from a political fight only makes us all more vulnerable. I don't get any pleasure out of saying this, but we live in a time where political bullying is the norm. We have to learn to fight back.

- Consequences matter. Many mistake good advocacy for big numbers and complicated analytics. The truth is that pain translated locally is more powerful if you hope to hold elected officials accountable.

THE THREE P'S FOR VOICES FOR NATIONAL SERVICE

Policy: Voices for National Service was founded to bring together all of the various groups and corps organized and funded under the CNCS banner (AmeriCorps, Senior Corps, Conservation Corps, VISTA, etc.). These entities engage in a fairly competitive process to see which corps and programs receive what allocations of money through competitive grants. They may be competitors for the final dollars but must work together annually on budgets and appropriations in order to secure the greatest levels of funding for the coalition overall. This is true not only when budgets are threatened, but also when political winds are more favorable and large gains can be made.

Once every ten years our work moves to reauthorizing the bill that allows CNCS to operate as an agency of the federal government. (The last reauthorization was in 2009 and was named in honor of Senator Edward M. Kennedy.) Our strategy for working the budget for CNCS spans a twenty-four-month calendar of activity beginning before the funds are ever allocated. That may seem a bit crazy, but the process is long, arduous, and competitive—even in good political times. Add opposition, as we've had for nearly a decade now, and the curve for success gets steeper and more harrowing.

Our process begins with CNCS as they prepare budget numbers and requests nearly two years before the money will flow. Then we work the White House to attempt to influence the president's budget with a favorable request for the agency. This process happens through the Office of Management and Budget. If the White House is for you, the process is easy, and the power of that recommended funding level is helpful. Sadly, the opposite is true, too.

Once the president's recommendations are sent to Capitol Hill, the House and Senate engage their respective budget committees to revise and amend the numbers, ending with a joint congressional budget resolution that sets the amounts, caps, and rules that the congressional appropriations committees can allocate for a fiscal year (this process is happening almost one year in advance of the actual spending). The appropriations committee then divides its work into thirteen subcommittees covering the entire federal government; those subcommittees have the power to put real numbers next to each agency's budget and line-item programs. The rubber really hits the road in these subcommittee deliberations. Since the House and Senate operate on parallel tracks, it is common for the subcommittees that decide on CNCS funding to come up with different numbers. Each chamber must then move the subcommittee bill to full committee and from full committee to the floor of the House and Senate. They are given the target date of October 1 each year to complete their work and pass bills that fund the country for the next full year. In recent times they've missed that deadline regularly, and continuing resolutions or threats to close down the government are becoming annual moments of crisis and concern. Our work is to track that process and make changes for the better at every step. If we aren't making progress, we're busy keeping cuts from destroying the work of the national service organizations on the ground trying to serve people and communities in need.

Politics: For many years CNCS enjoyed being the priority of the president and of a vast bipartisan majority in Congress. George H. W. Bush had begun the initial effort of what became CNCS in his inaugural address by calling for "a thousand points of light." It was established by President Clinton and grew and thrived. With the election of George W. Bush it grew further. Congressional champions as powerful and diverse as Senators Ted Kennedy, Orrin Hatch, and John McCain; Representatives Nancy Pelosi and Rosa DeLauro; and even Speaker John Boehner supported this agency and its programs. The community depended on this high-level support and the related advocacy effort was inside the Beltway, keeping friends and champions close and asking for favors in the critical moments.

Then came the Republican Tea Party phenomenon. The entire balance of bipartisanship and cooperation was upended. The politics went from consensual and cordial to tense and toxic in one election cycle. The new Republican chairman of the House Budget Committee, Paul Ryan, threatened CNCS with elimination—he actually proposed zero funding. In that moment, VNS knew it needed to drastically change course and reinvent its strategy. The Sheridan Group immediately recommended that CNCS take the fight to the local level. We knew members of Congress really care most about what happens at home. We threw ourselves into the districts where Appropriations Committee members were from. We found all the agencies that got any funding through CNCS, we contacted AmeriCorps alumni in those cities and states, and we talked to mayors, local celebrities, and church leaders. Our goal was to leave no stone unturned in making a local case for funding CNCS programs. Perhaps most important, we translated all the good these programs were doing and then made the absence of those good programs a direct consequence for the member if we lost. We did hundreds of pages of analysis to get data: if AmeriCorps were not in Joplin, Missouri, when a tornado struck, five thousand volunteers wouldn't have been on the streets that night providing emergency assistance, ten thousand hours of cleanup would not have happened, and hospitals would not have been able to transport patients to nearby undamaged hospitals without CNCS assistance. We got the frontpage of the Helena, Montana, newspaper to feature a photo of two older women working with Senior Corps stirring a cauldron of soup for needy seniors with the caption: "Congress threatens Senior Corps—these women's jobs and work will be lost." As soon as those tactics hit local areas, members began taking cover and opposing Paul Ryan. We won that fight in a remarkably quick and effective change of tactic from Beltway lobbying to local advocacy.

Paul Ryan not only kept his chairmanship of the House Budget Committee, he got promoted to Speaker of the House. Then Donald Trump got elected president, and in his first budget recommendation, he doubled down on Ryan's plan to zero out CNCS. We rallied again and made our positive case but also threatened accountability for the consequences of votes in favor of the Trump budget, and we won. As I write this, we are dealing with Trump's second budget. The blue wave did in fact sweep a leadership change into the House, and with it champions for national service are now in important and powerful positions as chairwomen of committees that matter to the future of CNCS. Trump is still president, and the Senate is still under Republican control, so our fight remains constant and bipartisan. The work never stops, especially in these politically challenging times.

Press: You have undoubtedly heard the expression "All politics is local." It was the favorite axiom of former Speaker of the House Tip O'Neill. What you may not know is that local politics is dictated by whatever is on the front page and editorial pages and websites of local newspapers. That's what members of Congress read first thing every morning. It's those pages that matter (no offense to the *New York Times*); the paper of record of any member is the local paper. Our press strategy mimicked this axiom. Local press, lots of it, and in any form we could create it.

This is not glamorous work. We wrote templates for letters to the editor so local folks could personalize them, sign them, and get them published. We trained our local advocates to schedule meetings with the local editorial board and pitch support for CNCS as a topic for them to write on. We helped create newsworthy events for local TV coverage. The CEO of the CNCS under Obama was a woman named Wendy Spencer (a lifelong Republican from Florida, by the way), who flew almost daily to communities across the country to highlight the work of CNCS and bring press attention with her. If a new Ameri-Corps award was being made in Kentucky where the Republican chairman of the House Appropriations Committee lived, she'd fly to meet him there to announce the new funding. It was hard, time-consuming work, but it achieved results. They say a picture is worth a thousand words, and when we staged that photo of older women stirring soup it garnered lots of attention and support. Press is a powerful amplification of your message and your value, and a great validator of your political power and support. It's essential to be aggressive with the press, but it need not be cost prohibitive. VNS certainly proved that point in their campaign to save CNCS and protect its funding. We're not done yet, but we are winning.

Epilogue

I FIRST CONCEIVED of the idea for this book as the culmination of twenty-five years of work with the Sheridan Group. Much of the writing took place in the waning months of the Obama presidency; I was optimistic about what the future would hold and what the Sheridan Group could achieve with Hillary Clinton as our next president. Now our country is in a vastly different place. The world feels fragile; the situation of our country dire. Yet it seems to me that the stories I have told in this book are even more important in these troubled times.

One week after the 2016 election, I was set to give the keynote speech at an annual convention for Independent Sector, a group often seen as the voice for the nation's non-profits. I had written the speech in some rare quiet moments in the fall of 2016, but after the election I knew I had to start again from scratch. Scott Fay, a vice president at the Sheridan Group, and Matt Schlesinger, an associate, struggled with me as I ping-ponged between despair and anger. The content and tone of the speech shifted hourly as I rapidly moved through phrases of grief and frustration. They hung in with me as we tried to put words and direction and emotion on paper.

As we worked on the speech I found myself thinking over the chapters of this book, looking for moments in the past when we had found hope in times of darkness. In a way, it was perfect timing for rethinking my talk; I had just spent months pulling together stories of successes in my career, victories that had sprung from worrisome times. I remembered the feelings I had when George H. W. Bush and then George W. Bush got elected and seemed to be poised to turn back the clock on many of the issues I'd championed and cared about, including cancer funding and LGBT rights. I remembered that out of very dark moments and moods we have found the strength and resilience to create some transformative moments in social policy—Ryan White is a perfect example.

What we eventually settled on for the speech was a direct and forceful political argument: in the face of adversity, the only choice is to stand up and fight back. There is no tougher audience than one that is anxious, depressed, and full of dread, but I wanted to confront them and challenge them, to push them to respond to the election results by going on the offensive through policy and advocacy. My point was clear: the nonprofit sector needs to offer leadership that brings the American public together. They are the sector that needs to step in with policy solutions and political pressure to ensure that the next four years are not as dark as our fears. I was walking a fine line; demoralized people rarely appreciate a confrontation, and the wounds of the election were still very fresh. But it was clear to me that there was, and still is, an opportunity for nonprofits to step up and start the work that can pull successes out of our defeat.

So while our current political situation is the polar opposite of what it was when I started writing, the same things are relevant. After all, this book is about the power of democracy; it's about the power of individuals to make change; it's about trusting yourself and your own power to engage with bold abandon in the messy and beautiful process of politics. These stories are my views on the change we envisioned and the processes we endured to try to make the world a slightly better place. This book is a collection of stories about people and issues that give voice and example to the spirit of America as an idea—something that keeps happening and changing, sometimes improving, sometimes not. Revolutions are never fought just by leaders; they are fought by many individuals who care deeply and passionately that change is needed, and who come up with solutions to inspire and create that change.

When I sat down to write this epilogue I asked my friend and collaborator what I should focus on. Her answer stopped me in my tracks: "Write about the purpose of your life's work," she offered, with a laugh. Seriously? I was stuck for weeks. How could I define my life's work when I see so much more work ahead? Summing up my work to date feels like writing my own epitaph—and that's not something I am ready to do. Yes, the 2016 election was incredibly disheartening, but I know I have more to do, more causes to fight for, more ideas to move into the forefront of the political dialogue. There is no way my life's work is complete. So instead of writing my own epitaph, I will leave you with this: If you picked up this book to learn how to help the good do better, I hope you are able to learn not only from my successes but also from my failures. I hope you see that even when our country's political scene is at its darkest, there is always hope. I promise you that I will keep working to make this country better for as long as it is possible, and I hope you will join me.

Acknowledgments

Peter and Josephine Sheridan: my parents, who died within eighteen months of each other and at critical stages of the book. The grief in these moments helped me tap into the love and inspiration that propels my work. Their belief in me gave me hope that making a positive change in the world truly is possible. They were both conservative Republicans, and because of that, I have often stopped in more heated moments to remember that my "opponents" in an advocacy effort are often "just like my parents." This may sound odd, but it cools it off a bit and allows me to behave a bit more civilly. Our family debates always provided me with powerful "opposition research." My siblings: Peter T. Sheridan, Cathy and John Lawlor, Ann Sheridan, and Maureen Sheridan remain the core of our family unit, and while we are all vastly different, we find our commonality in the love and comfort of each other's company. In politics I sometimes observe the familiar patterns of families, particularly large boisterous Irish families: We can fight and argue; love, laugh, and cry; but in the end, we are always committed to pulling together. I thank them for the constants they provide for me in life. We need to treat our political culture a little more like a family. My nieces and nephews: Jack, Cara, Colleen, and Tyler are the future of the nation and will be part of a generation poised to deliver big change. On the tough days I keep going because I believe in their future more than our past. The extended family owns a piece of all that I am and what I bring because with them I have learned to see the world from angles I might not have witnessed had they not shared their joys, sorrows, challenges, and perspectives. The Desmonds, McAndrews, Bigginses, Mahedys, Granard Sheridans, and Ballinrobe Murphy all have my gratitude. If you've read the book, then you already know that "Nana" (aka Mary Ellen Biggins née Murphy) was our matriarch and my inspiration for following this rather unusual path in life.

Pat Christen, Rene Durazzo, and Kim McCleary: These three individuals were the first to believe in the idea of the Sheridan Group. They were my first clients, who took a giant leap of faith, and suffered some criticisms, in the notion of a firm dedicated to "helping the good do better." Those first years were formative and remain foundational to the values the firm holds dear even through today. I consider the three of them dear friends for life.

The "Mentors": For too many reasons to detail, and risking the fact I know I'll not get this list to be exhaustive and complete, the following people provided friendship, inspiration, advice, mentorship, confidence, and criticism that propelled my work and filled my soul over this journey: Mary I. DiFonzo, Kathy Foley, Suzanne Ball, Msgr. Robert Ritchie, Lorraine Voles, Walter Mondale, Paul Tully, Mike and Sally Ford, Tom Cosgrove, Steve Elmendorf, David Liederman, Senator and Vicki Kennedy, Jean McGuire, Jeanne White, Speaker Nancy Pelosi, Bono, Jamie Drummond, Bobby Shriver, Diane Canova, Bill Novelli, Fr. Tim Scully, Congresswoman Rosa DeLauro, Mary McDonough, Sybil Goldrich, Pam Omidyar, Mark Shriver, Betsy Zorio, Amy Fulford, Rebecca Bagley, Mike Cassidy, Keith Cylar, Mike Shriver, Pat Griffin, Sonal Shah, Cheryl Dorsey, Paul Schmidt, Jim and Patti Doyle, Senator Chris Coons, Michael Paese, Tom Fry, Sandy Thurman, and Senator Harris Wofford. To refrain from duplications, anyone mentioned in the chapters of this book would fairly fit into this category as well.

Shannon O'Neill: A collaborator of first-rate quality and character, she wrote, edited, and researched above and beyond the call of duty. When life got rough during patches of writing this book, it was Shannon who pulled it through. It's not an exaggeration—this book would not have been written without her.

Sean Desmond: For believing in this idea from the beginning, for trusting my contribution to making change, and for supporting me through the many ups and downs of writing a book and getting it published.

Bridgit Matzie: An early supporter who brought Shannon to the team, brokered the final publishing deal, and otherwise acted as a kind and thoughtful coach along the way.

Ruby Marie Smith: Our amazing goddaughter, passionate reader, and talented literary genius. I only gave this book in its manuscript form to one person to read—she loved it, and now it's real.

The team at Twelve: For all the little things they did to support and guide a new author on his first venture.

The team at TSG: This book was nearly ten years in the making. Many members of the TSG team (present and alumni) contributed to the work that is recorded here over those years, but they also contributed to the effort to actually write the book, time spent in addition to the day-to-day work of the firm. This crew of dedicated professionals picked up the slack, ventured into some unfamiliar waters, and supported the idea of this book without complaint or compromise. After more than twenty-five years in the business of advocacy and change, I would put the present team at TSG and our alumni among the proudest of my achievements.

TSG clients, past, present, and future: You are only as good as the clients who entrust you to work with and lead them on the path to social change. I am fortunate to have had nearly three decades in business with truly amazing people and causes. Some have been wildly successful and long term, others have tried and failed, but each has been a member of the "family" and nearly all are considered friends to this day. It's a privilege to show up for work respecting and admiring the people you work for. I'm grateful for it every day.

Second View Authors: This was a novel idea and not necessarily an easy ask of colleagues and friends. I gave them little guidance other than "tell the unvarnished truth from your perspective and tell it to teach." Their smart, insightful, honest perspectives added deep value to the book.

Kristin O'Connell Upton and Jesse Torrence: This book tried for takeoff twice prior to its actual flight. The first time Kristin sorted through files, researched, organized, and helped me dig into my memories of the events included here. The second go-round brought Jesse to the team for an intense summer of interviews, writing, and researching. I'm grateful to them both, and the final product directly benefited from their early efforts.

Index

About the Author

Thomas F. Sheridan is the nation's foremost advocate for public interest causes and social impact. His career spans more than thirty years and has touched nearly all of the transformative social issues of our time, both domestically and internationally. From the AIDS pandemic with Bono to twenty-first-century social innovation, Thomas has used his heart and his head to lead successful strategies that have changed the world. He is a social worker by profession and a rare "white hat" lobbyist by trade. Thomas is married to Vince Walsh. They live in Washington, DC and Lewes, DE, with their three pets: Phina, Duffy, and Ryan.